HOW WE MET

Michèle A'Court is a stand-up comedian and writer, and the bestselling author of *Stuff I Forgot To Tell My Daughter* (HarperCollins, 2015). Mother of one and grandmother of two remarkably beautiful and gifted people, she lives in Auckland with her third and final husband.

HOW WE MET

the ways great love begins...

MICHELE A'COURT

HarperCollinsPublishers

HarperCollins*Publishers*

First published in 2018
by HarperCollins*Publishers* (New Zealand) Limited
Unit D1, 63 Apollo Drive, Rosedale, Auckland 0632, New Zealand
harpercollins.co.nz

HarperCollins*Publishers*
Unit D1, 63 Apollo Drive, Rosedale, Auckland 0632, New Zealand
Level 13, 201 Elizabeth Street, Sydney NSW 2000, Australia
A 53, Sector 57, Noida, UP, India
1 London Bridge Street, London, SE1 9GF, United Kingdom
2 Bloor Street East, 20th floor, Toronto, Ontario M4W 1A8, Canada
195 Broadway, New York NY 10007, USA

A catalogue record for this book is available from
the National Library of New Zealand

ISBN 978 1 7755 4093 9 (pbk)
ISBN 978 1 7754 9131 6 (ebook)

Cover design by Holly Dunn
Front cover photo by Kate Little, Kate Little Photography
Typeset in Sabon LT Std by Kirby Jones
Author photograph by Kate Little, Kate Little Photography
Printed and bound in Australia by McPhersons Printing Group
The papers used by HarperCollins in the manufacture of this book are a natural, recyclable product made from wood grown in sustainable plantation forests. The fibre source and manufacturing processes meet recognised international environmental standards, and carry certification.

For Jeremy.

(Pleased I met you.)

And for my parents, Donna and John.

(Pleased you met.)

Contents

INTRODUCTION

'So, How Did You Two Meet?'

IT'S THE QUESTION EVERYONE gets around to asking a couple eventually. What brought you together? How did you find each other? Where does the story of the two of you begin? In the right moment with the right people, you get to sit back and hear a heartwarming tale about how two humans discovered each other. And if you are watching carefully as they tell it — taking turns, laughing together, adding their favourite details — it might occur to you that if you want to see two people at their best and closest, ask them to describe the moment they fell in love.

Which is exactly how this book started. One story told over dinner in July 2015 by a pair of friends I'd known for a while, about how they had fallen for each other 19 years before. I watched them sparkle as they told a tale that starred the two of them, and I swear it was like watching them fall in love again. And suddenly that night, a big shiny universal theory hit me quite hard: these stories we all adore about how couples meet — the romantic, absurd, serendipitous, convoluted, scandalous, breath-taking moments of connection — help to weave our lives together. Partly as 'proof' that we were meant to begin this couple-journey, and also because in each retelling we go back to those first falling-in-love feelings and rekindle the passion.

Here, at the beginning, my theory is based on a hunch, which itself is based on nothing more than my observations of couples as they talk. I'm keen to ask as many couples as I can if my wild theory resonates with them — to run it up a metaphorical flagpole and see who salutes; and I will hold it in the back of my mind as I watch their faces and listen to their voices. I also want to try out my crazy thesis on a neuroscientist and a psychologist. And, by the end of the book, I hope to have some useful things to say not only about the ways great love starts, but how it stays great.

Telling these stories is, I'd argue, not just good for the people *in* the stories, but also good for *all* of us to hear. For a start, they're gorgeous little vignettes, complete in themselves from 'once upon a time' to 'happily ever after'. And we've been gobbling up 'falling-in-love' stories since the dawn of time — from movies, books and songs right back through fairy tales, chronicles, legends and myths. They give us hope that they'll happen to us, or affirm that they've *already* happened to us.

Amid the chaos of living on a planet with 7 billion people, they suggest there might be sufficient magic floating around for us to find the one person we truly belong with, our One In Particular. Or at least (hello, cynics) to find a person with whom we can happily keep weaving our life together for as long as we both want.

CHAPTER 1

How I Met This Book

THERE IS A THEORY that you meet the right person only when you stop looking for them. I can't say that's entirely true, but I do think you often find the best *ideas* when you're not looking for them. Empty your head, make a space, and something lovely turns up.

It is the middle of winter at home in New Zealand, and so my husband, Jeremy, and I have run off to Rarotonga for a few days to Stop Thinking. My brain is fried from writing and touring, so we've given ourselves five days to disconnect — no emails, no newspapers, no writing, no deadlines, no planning. Just swimming with the fishes, whale-spotting from the shoreline, and afternoon cocktails. Sometimes I sit with a thoroughly good book in my lap for several hours without turning a page. My single goal is to perfect my ability to float a cocktail — a game I'd invented there six months earlier, where you sit yourself waist-deep in the lagoon, plop a large glass filled with some kind of fruity, boozy concoction into the water in front of you, let it find its equilibrium, and then drink it very slowly through a straw without using your hands. It isn't necessarily going well — the wind is up and the waves make it hazardous. But everyone needs a project, and this is mine.

The only other thing I am prepared to commit to is dinner at The Waterline, our favourite beachside bar and grill. Sunset here feels like a show. People stop talking to watch it.

Tradition has it that this dinner will be with Ian and Clare, an English couple who have lived on the island since 2007. We'd first met them five years earlier at this exact spot — two pairs of strangers then, seated at separate tables. But by the end of that evening we'd all bonded over great food, lashings of booze, and the late-night jam session it had morphed into. Tama, the son of The Waterline's owner, Chris, provides the official musical entertainment, but at some point the local diners had insisted that Chris get his guitar out, too. Then it turned out that Ian plays guitar, and Jeremy always has a mouth-harp in his pocket, and they all knew the same songs. So Ian had pitched in, and Jeremy joined them, and everyone sang a few, and delightful mayhem ensued. The quiet diners drifted off, more wine was bought, and it evolved into a party. Which is how we first got talking to Ian and Clare.

More random encounters: it seemed that every time we visited the island we would bump into Ian and Clare — the Fates were throwing us together. No matter what time of year we went, or which night we picked for dinner at The Waterline, there they would be — we couldn't tell who was stalking whom, but we all found it hilarious. The guitars and harmonicas would come out, and we were always the last to leave the bar. Eventually, we swapped contact details, so by the time we were having dinner in July 2015, a booking had been made specifically for our party of four.

And then, five years after we first met, in a natural lull between the steak (house speciality) and the jam session (guest speciality), I asked the inevitable question: So, how did you two meet? Together, they told this hilarious yarn about Clare falling down a hole in a kebab shop; and they laughed, and we laughed, and they took turns to tell different bits, and finished each other's sentences, and it was highly entertaining and made all of us feel good about the world.

And then I said, 'That's a great story! I love hearing stories like that. Someone should write a book about those kinds of stories.' And we all agreed, and then the three of them looked at me, and I thought about it for a minute and said, 'Okay, I will then.' And here we are.

CHAPTER 2

Falling Down a Hole in a Kebab Shop

IAN WAS 22 YEARS OLD and Clare was 24 when they went out for a kebab in Derby, England. Clare is a tiny slip of a thing, and Ian is a tall man built like a whippet. To fill in the gaps of my own hazy memories from our dinner at The Waterline, I asked **Clare and Ian Wheeldon** to tell me their story again. They waited until the end of their working week, went home and opened a bottle of wine, and then Ian sent this email from Rarotonga.

> *Clare and I knew each other from the club I used to DJ in, The Blue Note in Derby. Clare was the 'Indie Kid', and I was a 'Crusty' who all her friends frowned at. Years go by with lots of flirting when Clare wanted her songs played. Eventually Clare ends up working behind the bar. So lots more flirting.*

Friday, 24 May 1996

8.30pm

I was playing in a rubbish band and had a gig at a local bar. Clare had her friend visiting from Manchester, and dragged the poor bugger along to see us. Let's be clear: Clare was not at all interested in the band. After the gig, I invited them both back to my house to have a few vodkas and meet the pet snakes and the cat.

10.00pm

After several drinks at my house we all headed out to the local nightclub. Neither of us actually remembers what happened to Clare's friend, Bruce. We do know we ended up sitting on the edge of a dirty dancefloor, snogging.

2.30am

At the end of the night, drunk and hungry, we headed for the nearest takeaway in Derby town centre. Our mutual friend and my housemate, Gaz Thatch, was with us because I'd always buy him a pizza. When we arrived at the takeaway, the hatch in the floor down to the cellar was open, with a gate around it. Unfortunately, a fight suddenly broke out and everyone got shoved around. Being too drunk and happy to care, I didn't pay too much attention, but all of a sudden Gaz Thatch was pointing down the steps to the cellar and telling the staff: 'No, honestly, she's really down there.'

It turns out that Clare had actually been pushed down the hole during the kafuffle, but fortunately was too drunk and floppy to sustain any serious injury other than a bit of a sore leg. She was actually quite lucky, as it was a good 10-foot drop. The staff of the takeaway didn't believe anyone had fallen down there, hence my friend's protestations.

Even though Clare's flat was closest, I thought it better that she come to my house so I could 'keep an eye' on her. I piggybacked her the mile or so to my house, both of us laughing all the way. It was no bother, Clare's only little.

After she got the taxi of shame back home the next morning, we kept the whole thing pretty quiet, but kept on seeing each other. What was really supposed to be a one-night-stand carried on and on.

10 August 2001

Eloped to Hawaii.

May 2007

Moved to Rarotonga.

Friday, 4 November 2016: 9.30pm

Still drunk, still in love in paradise. And we meet some really interesting people!

There are so many things to love about this story. There's the specificity: the detailed timeline, the snakes, the vodka, the state of the dancefloor, Gaz Thatch and his penchant for pizza. And the dramatic visuals of a fight breaking out and Clare on the periphery getting nudged over and falling through a trapdoor, and then Gaz trying to convince everyone it really had happened. It's like a great grown-up cartoon.

And also the sense that Ian and Clare had been dancing around each other for ages — two kids from different tribes trying to resist the pull — until enough vodka and a pash got them to a place where the Fates made it possible for them to finally, literally, fall for each other.

It also has the feel of a story told many times over the years — that's how you remember those kind of details, right? By telling the story regularly — not necessarily to other people, but certainly to each other — from quite soon after it happened when the memories are fresh, and then again as the years go by, bedding in the specifics. And then the general sense of joy from both of them that something random happened — the fight and the fall — which set them on a path that they're thrilled with.

I love the way they've recorded it here — Ian as narrator, with Clare chipping in, wine in hand — but I also loved the way they told it together, the 'live' version at dinner in 2015. They took turns then, telling different bits, but the overwhelming impression was that they were telling the story, not to us, but to each other.

So having gone to Rarotonga specifically *not* looking for an idea, I came home with an idea I was dying to write about — the ways great love begins, and what makes it stay great. Because from time to time, love needs all the help it can get.

CHAPTER 3

Hatching and Matching

HERE'S WHY WE NEED stories. Life — as far as I can tell after half-a-century of it — is chaos. There's no grand plan, and no one running the show. (I totally appreciate not everyone feels like this, but run with me for a moment.) And because life is unpredictable and messy, each of us tries to make sense of this chaos by constructing a narrative that gives it shape. Glorious things and shitty things happen, and then, as soon as we can, we find a way to talk about them that gives them meaning and value.

Think about some big event in your life — let's say the birth of a child. When it is happening, it doesn't feel like a story; it's a bunch of moments involving different locations, physical experiences, various characters coming in and out, many different kinds of words spoken, and a wide range of emotions. At the time, it doesn't feel like a beautifully crafted scene in a movie, right? But sometime around the point you hold that baby in your arms, you start to make their arrival on the planet into a story. You choose where the story begins — maybe when the waters broke, maybe as far back as conception — and you find the things that make it special or beautiful or portentous and, often, by the time the first visitors arrive you can tell them some lovely tale about how this all happened, how this new person made their entrance, who they look like, what kind of person they already are. From all those random events — a meal you'd just cooked but didn't get to eat, a storm, a cancelled flight, the cat bringing in a bird, the song that was playing on the way to the hospital in the car, what the midwife was wearing, whatever — you choose which of those elements helps to tell your story, and let the other details fall away. And the Birth Story is the beginning of you bonding with this new person and weaving them into your life.

My mother was very ill when I was born, and so those first few days of my life are a blur to her. But she loves to tell the bit about when she and I came home from the hospital, and my brother, Stephen, then two-and-a-half, would greet visitors at the front door, take them by the hand, lead them towards my bedroom and say, 'Come and see my baby.' Not 'the baby' or even 'my sister' — I was the baby who belonged particularly to him. That's not the only reason my brother and I have always been so close, but my mother repeating that story to me from as long ago as I can remember is certainly a part of it. That little story — which was just about him and me — bound us together from the start.

So couples, then, and their stories. Couples need stories because, let's be honest, relationships are effing hard. Or maybe it's not that relationships are hard, but that life is. In the beginning it's all about the two of you, and you are both suddenly new and exciting (to yourselves and each other) and life is full of discovery and frisson and thrill. You talk about music and books, and see movies and discuss big ideas and introduce each other to new things, and food tastes better and the sun shines brighter, and you sniff their clothes when the other person is not there and marvel that no one has bottled this scent because it is how the whole world should smell. Then at some point, instead of finding each other endlessly fascinating, the two of you are having business meetings about who's picking up the kids, and should you fix or float the mortgage, and for God's sake if you knew we were out of milk why didn't you get some? And it's hard to feel romantic when you've spent part of your day scraping whatever that was off the toilet bowl, and have you taken the bins out because it's Tuesday again and why doesn't Tuesday set off a 'bins' alarm in your head, and something weird happened at the team meeting today and Brian gave me a look I can't fathom and none of your questions are helping and I think the kid's wet the bed.

Jeremy and I call this 'poo through the windows'. Both of us quite regularly find that we visualise our lives as the two of us sitting happily with each other in our little house surrounded by books and all the things we've brought home from the places we visit, having a perfectly lovely time together, and then some third party (and often a fourth and fifth) sneaks up to the windows and chucks poo at us that we then have to deal with. External pressures, other people's stuff. It is possible, while you are dealing with the poo, to lose sight of your partner and what they're doing to deal with the poo themselves. Or you are so mad (or sad, or just exhausted) by the poo, that this feeling spills over to the way you treat your partner, and you forget that the poo isn't theirs and that they didn't throw it, and then also forget to be kind to them. Or you forget what life was like pre-poo, or even why you were sitting in the room with them in the first place. And then you're not in a living room anymore, you're drowning in an ocean of poo, each of you struggling to keep your heads above it, and the storm is raging and you lose sight of one another and you're in big trouble.

So you need a lifejacket and a whistle. Something to buoy you up, and to signal to each other. 'I'm over here! It's me! Remember me?' That's what couples' stories are for.

As social creatures, we've always recognised this need to create and sustain a shared story. This has got to be one of the major reasons that humans invented The Wedding. Sure, The Wedding is about making sure the whole village is cognisant of the fact that Sherryl and David are now an official thing — hands off, everyone else. And it is also a bringing together of Shaz's and Dave's families and land and cows — or whatever the equivalent might be today. And yes, it is also an opportunity for any number of drunk uncles to make twats of themselves on the dancefloor or blow the dust off casually racist and homophobic jokes, for bridesmaids to make a play for the groom's brother, for aunts to ask inappropriate questions about when older siblings are going to settle down and/or produce tiny feet that patter, and general embarrassment over bouquet tossing and appalling speeches from groomsmen detailing events that should never be spoken of in public, and for someone to drunkenly stumble far too close to the three-tier cake. All of that, yes. But it is also an event taking a day — in some cultures more — to celebrate these two people and make them the stars of a romantic scene. Music, flowers, vows, speeches, frocks, suits, entertainment — all captured in photos, recorded in videos, and held in the minds of witnesses from which stories will later be told.

When I was a kid it was likely that, in any house I went to, the oldest photograph on display of the resident couple (and therefore them at their youngest and most vigorous) would be their wedding photo. Their first 'together' photo. It quietly suggested: 'This is where our story begins, on this day.' Back then, there were no pictures on the walls of their pre-wedding coupledom — no skiing holidays or camping trips or dances. It's different now, because we tend to marry later on in the relationship, or don't marry at all. (Plus we take photos of everything — brunch, for example — not just things that matter.) But still, even now, The Wedding is sometimes our first big shared story.

And we didn't just invent The Wedding, we invented The Wedding Anniversary. Anniversaries aren't just a test of memory (though they're also that) or a moment to prove you're still into it (ditto) or an excuse to splash out on that coffee machine you both wanted (fair call). This is society suggesting to us that once a year we need to say, 'Hey, let's take a moment to remember where we started, what we dreamed of, who we were when we leapt off this lovely cliff.'

The Wedding and The Anniversary might be conscious social constructs, but it happens organically, too. Lots of couples who feel really good about their 'How We Met' story mark that anniversary as well. Ian and Clare are prime examples — they have two anniversaries a year. One on 24 May, 'for when we first got it on' as Ian so eloquently puts it, and another for their August wedding. Always a good excuse, they both agree, for a party.

'Having a story' isn't restricted to weddings or first meetings — all it really needs is some drama that involves you both. It can even happen at a baseball game …

CHAPTER 4

Seventh-inning Stretch

ANDREW AND HEATHER got engaged at Yankee Stadium in New York on 27 September 2016. I know this because my husband is a massive baseball fan (we support the Los Angeles Angels of Anaheim at our place), and we had the Yankees versus Red Sox game playing in our living room that day.

One of the glorious things about baseball is that it's not just about the baseball. There's on-field entertainment — singers, flyovers, presentations to community heroes — and hilarious between-innings distractions like 'kiss cam' where images of couples are projected onto the big screen and the audience encourages them to kiss. Weird if you're sitting with your brother, but the camera operators mostly pick appropriate people.

During the middle of the fifth inning (that's about halfway through the game), the capacity crowd at Yankee Stadium — and viewers at home — saw a shot of Andrew and Heather on the Jumbotron. On cue, Andrew got down on one knee and took a ring box out of his pocket, and asked Heather to marry him. But then — as the crowd held its collective breath — Andrew fumbled and dropped the ring. The crowd gasped, then jeered the fumble, then watched transfixed as everyone near the couple searched frantically under their seats. After an excruciatingly long time — close to five actual human minutes, much of it with running commentary from the TV hosts — Heather noticed something glinting in the cuff of her trousers. There was an announcement over the PA to confirm that the ring had been found and the crowd went wild. Andrew dropped to his knee again and proposed. 'That is awesome!' the television commentator declared. 'Oh, she *better* say yes!' And she did — with a long kiss and an even longer hug. 'I'm saying,' the commentator continued, 'you always want a story. Well ... they got a story!' Thirty-five thousand fans gave the couple a standing ovation. Minutes later, Heather and Andrew were named 'Fans of the Day' and could be spotted in cutaway shots for the remainder of the game giving interviews to various media organisations. They were already telling their Proposal Story. Even now, the footage makes me weep happy tears.

So yeah, the dude is right: you've got to have a story. The engagement, the wedding, the birth of a child. But it seems there might be a particularly potent magic infused into the stories of how people meet. Each time you go back and describe how you met your One In Particular you are doing two powerful things: offering up a kind of proof that you are meant to be together; and also reigniting those first falling-in-love feelings and rekindling the flames.

Back home from Rarotonga in 2015, I did a shout-out on social media (Facebook and Twitter), asking people to get in touch with me with their stories.

> *Hello, everyone. I am writing a new book which will be in large part a collection of 'How We Met' stories — those lovely stories couples love to tell (and we all love to hear) about how they got together. At this point, I am keen to get in touch with couples who have been together for 15 years or more about their romantic / funny / bizarre / surprising / delightful answer to, 'So how did you two meet?' Email me at …*

Now, I should explain the 15-year thing. It was an arbitrary rule (and, indeed, I have broken it a few times), but there was some thinking behind it. First, I wanted couples who had met pre-Tinder (2012), and even before internet dating was a thing. Not that either of those ways of meeting aren't valid — they definitely are, and actually you'll find a couple of those stories here, too. (Yeah, yeah, I know — another arbitrary rule gets kicked into touch.) Involving a touch (or swipe) of technology doesn't negate romance or frisson, and we'll get better at appreciating that as the years go by. Someone told me about a couple who had met on Tinder but skipped that detail from their 'How We Met' story at their wedding because they were worried great-aunts and grandpas would disapprove. That'll change.

But, to begin with, I wanted some version of 'hot bodies in a room' with all the senses engaged. Touch and smell as well as sound and vision. (Possibly taste if it came up, but I wasn't going to raise it first.) So those physical connections in the real world, where no one was necessarily looking for anyone but some random encounter led to something fully life-changing.

My instinct told me that 15 years was a good yardstick for measuring that a relationship was pretty settled. It is possible that it all goes tits-up after that point, of course — I hope we all know the fabulous Irish joke about the couple in their nineties who go to the parish priest for an annulment after having been miserable for 75 years, but they'd felt it was best to stay together until all their kids were dead. Ba ha ha ha ha.

To the naked eye, it seems lots of human endeavours go in cycles of seven. It takes seven years for your body to renew every cell, for example — which means in 2018 you are a completely different person, physically, from the one you were in 2011. Leaf through a pile of CVs and you'll see a striking number of people find the seventh year a good time to move on to the next job. In baseball, there's a firm tradition of getting the crowd up and moving in the middle of the seventh inning because everyone knows that's when attention and energy might wane. You grab a hotdog and a beer, and join in a charming group singalong of 'Take Me Out to the Ballgame' during the 'seventh-inning stretch'. And of course, reaching a relationship use-by date a bit after half-a-dozen years is common enough for us to have a name for it: 'the seven-year itch'.

So I figured surviving two-cycles-of-seven-plus-a-bonus-year meant you'd learned a couple of things, and pretty much decided to give it a jolly good crack. There is this lovely, mature moment in a relationship — which might come earlier or later for different people — when you take 'I could just bugger off' off the table and start throwing down 'Let's sort this out because you're fundamentally awesome and I couldn't be arsed breaking in anyone new.' Something like that, anyway.

An arbitrary 15-year rule then, broken a few times, with delightful results.

Very quickly after my social media shout-out, the good people at RNZ National heard what I was up to and invited me into the studio to chat on-air to get the word out further. Over the next few days my inbox filled up with stories. People telling their own or their parents' stories, or dobbing in their mates.

They were excited and enthusiastic. Occasionally they were a little diffident and self-deprecating:

> 'Fairly sure that this is not exciting enough but ...'
>
> 'I don't know if our story is exactly what you're looking for ... but ...'
>
> 'I've been with my husband for 41 years ... Is that too long?'

But often proud:

> 'I have what I think is a great story ...'
>
> 'I quite like our narrative, if I may say so myself.'
>
> 'We've only been together 10 years, but it's a pretty cool story ...'

And men wrote to me almost as often as women:

> 'My beautiful wife, Julie, and I met in the early months of 1992 ...'
>
> 'I have been with my beautiful wife 22 years ...'

The even gender-split surprised me in the beginning, but it shouldn't have. I've thought about that a lot since. I'm used to women telling women personal and intimate stories about their lives, even when we don't know each other well, or at all. And of course I have proper, meaningful chats with close male friends. This, however, was a shout-out to strangers, and I hadn't expected men I didn't know to open up so readily and trust me with their personal tales. I mentioned this to Jeremy one evening, and he was surprised that I was surprised. Men in long-term relationships, he says, are proud of it and like to talk about it. It's an achievement. Just to meet a woman, he says, men need to be creative. 'If a woman wants a man to talk to her in a bar, all she has to do is wait. But a man could sit there forever.' (There are probably legions of women who will describe this phenomenon differently — mostly about the *kind* of man she meets in a bar — but I appreciate his point.)

Something I really have noticed is that there is nothing a woman finds more attractive than a man who is passionately and faithfully in love with his partner. Hear a dude talk adoringly about the woman he loves and the ladies listening get a little bit hot for him. And you can ponder the irony of that for as long as you want.

So these stories don't belong to one person, they belong to two. They celebrate both partners — the risks they took, their leaps of faith, their courage and tenacity. There's hunting and being chased — and, hilariously, often different perspectives on who did which. Yet in every story *both* partners are the stars — two active participants — and so they're equally willing to do the telling.

All of the stories made me smile; some of them made me laugh; now and then I'd tear-up a bit; and more than once I heard myself say out loud to my computer screen, 'Aww ...' It occurred to me that my inbox was pretty much the exact opposite of Nicky Hager's when he was writing *Dirty Politics*. Dozens of emails showing how good and kind and open people are. I replied to as many of them as I could, and started looking for patterns that might make sense of the delightful chaos of my inbox.

I have arranged them throughout the book by themes, or the flavour of each story: love-at-first-sight, hate-at-first-sight, catastrophic beginnings, pairs of people who took forever to get it together for God's sake, or couples who instantly took massive risks to be together. Sometimes, though, I've used the same instincts I apply as a comedy-show MC choosing the order of performers, and arranged things in terms of the story I think you might like to hear next. But before we go looking for commonalities or contrasts, let's just dive into a bunch of wildly different examples of how people meet.

CHAPTER 5

'It Must Have Been the Kiss'

MANY COUPLES CAN TELL their stories with tremendous simplicity: two people, unencumbered, delivered by the Fates to the same location and — *bam!* — there's a metaphorical lightning-bolt, or a glass-slipper-moment, or a really great actual kiss. Put them on the spot and they can give you the romantic equivalent of an elevator pitch. Ask a couple in the front row of a comedy show how they met, and you might be lucky enough to get 'At a pizza shop in Ecuador — I'd been backpacking through Peru and she was on a study exchange from Minnesota. We've been together ever since — she won't go home because of Trump.' True story.

Here are some more …

*

Antarctica, 2001: Ronlyn was working at Casey Station when

a gang of the girls decided it would be fun to have a mock hen's night. You make your own fun in the Arctic circles.

> *I volunteered to be the bride (36 ... desperate) and then we went about looking for a groom. My now-husband, Arthur, happened to walk through the door as we all turned our attention to who that should be, and so he was chosen. He was a willing participant. We got married at 10pm that night (mucking around as you do in Antarctica). I was wearing a duvet cover as a veil somehow wrapped around my head, and the station leader read out the vows that the girls had written out earlier on a paper table cloth — we'd mulled it over during dinner in preparation after telling Arthur he was getting married. Thoughtfully, he arrived with rings (the usual can ring-pull but beautifully decorated with a strip of brass for me, and a brass nut for him). Having got married, we then got to know each other and the rest is history. It must have been the kiss.*
>
> *We did get married officially in a forest in Tasmania in 2009. The ceremony was somewhat confusing for our five-year-old daughter, as we'd always told her we had got married in Antarctica — because we did!*
>
> — **Ronlyn Duncan,** *Christchurch.*

Later, I asked Ronlyn whether she and Arthur still have the rings, and whether they celebrate both of their anniversaries, or just one. 'I still have the ring-pull ring, but the nut went back to the workshop, I understand. Arthur doesn't wear rings, so it was very sweet that he thought to get one for the wedding. I think he had help. Which anniversary do we celebrate? We're terrible at that stuff but, of course, we should be celebrating both. From this year forward ...'

*

I met my wife when she was the queen in our medieval re-enactment group visiting from LA. I was her queen's guard. She now lives in NZ and it's our 12th wedding anniversary on Sunday.

*— **Alasdair**, Auckland*

*

I always say I won my husband in a raffle. I was working as a nurse on a surgical ward, and in the morning report the night nurses said there was a doctor admitted overnight. No one wanted to look after him. We drew straws and I got the short straw. We have been married 11 years and have two children and a dog now ...

— **Fiona**

*

My best friend's folks are called Faye and Dave. They met at a party. Faye was sitting on the floor. Dave trod across her fingers. They've been together for more than 50 years and are an utter delight.

— **Beck Eleven**, Christchurch

*

In the kitchen at a party in Notting Hill a woman with a Bic biro pinned through her hair knot (she looks interesting) swapped numbers, wrote her phone number on a teabag, the only paper to hand. Knowing from experience that if you meet someone you like in London, get their number, because in a city of 12 million people YOU WILL NEVER SEE THEM AGAIN. I called her the next day, she's not interested.

I made a cup of tea with the bag and mentally moved on, but I got a call back a few days later — married 20 years, two boys, 18 and 16.

— **Tony Richards**, Auckland

*

My wife and I met in London, on the day of the Oxford–Cambridge Boat Race in 1997. We both came from Christchurch and had mutual friends and lived around the corner from each other, but had never met in Christchurch. Had to travel halfway around the world to meet each other. We were married in 2004 and have two beautiful kids.

— **Richard McCormick**, Christchurch

*

You can also fall in love in your own backyard. At an afternoon event I was speaking at in 2017, they seated me next to a delightful woman, **Joyce Irving**. At 96 years old, Joyce had spent a lifetime on the stage, had starred in her first short film, *Dotty*, aged 91, and still makes the odd television commercial. Currently, she told me, she was in one for life insurance, holding up a piece of knitting with the company's name crafted into it — although she wouldn't take the credit for that. 'I didn't do the knitting myself,' she said. 'Ah, a prop,' I said, and she seemed pleased I was using the proper term. I admired her scarf — a delicate, floaty thing in pale green — and she told me that, when she dies, her whole scarf collection will be brought to the funeral so people can take one home with them. 'What a lovely memento of you,' I said, 'to have you wrapped around them.' She agreed, but insisted she couldn't take the credit for that either — New Zealand theatre and literary doyen Rosalie Carey, Joyce's contemporary, had arranged this for her funeral six years ago, and Joyce had admired it.

She asked what I was up to, and I told her about this book. Joyce offered her own story. Her first husband had died in 1981, and she'd met her second husband a couple of years later when he'd called out to her over their shared garden fence: 'Would you like some new potatoes?'

'You can guess the answer,' she twinkled. So they were the first words from Jim, husband number two. Eight-and-a-half years later, when he was dying, Jim's daughter came to be with them both. After sitting at his bedside for a while, the daughter joined Joyce in the kitchen and told her, 'Dad says the last eight-and-a-half years have been the happiest of his life.' Sitting at our table now, Joyce looked proud and satisfied. *This* was the thing she would take credit for. And then, before we all left, she said, with more twinkling, 'Number three hasn't found me yet.'

*

Some of the tales take longer than your average elevator ride to tell, but they come with the exact time and location of two souls colliding, and tiny details recalled.

In 1979, **Mary** arrived in New Zealand from Washington state, got lost in downtown Auckland and was rescued by **Morri**, a friendly bus driver. They married two years later, and now have a couple of grown-up kids. This is their story involving perms, the Topp Twins, and a superb pick-up line.

> *After two years of teaching primary school in a 'rural ghetto' in Idaho, I was ready for adventure, so I decided to go around the world all by myself, even though I had hardly ever travelled before. My first planned stop was Bali, where I heard one could live in a hut on the beach for a dollar a day. The travel agent explained that I would first have to travel to this country called New Zealand, make my way over to Darwin, Australia, and then fly up to Bali from there.*

I had 'friends of friends' to stay with in New Zealand, so off I flew to Auckland via Pago Pago. My first day in New Zealand and I promptly got lost in downtown Auckland. I couldn't figure out how to get back to my youth hostel, and I didn't know that I was supposed to wave down a bus if I wanted it to stop for me. I stood at a street corner looking disoriented enough for a friendly ARA bus driver to shout out from his bus, 'Whereabouts are you going?' I had just enough time to weave my way through traffic and hop on his bus before the lights changed and he drove off.

He was 6 foot 7 inches tall, had crinkly, smiling eyes, long curly hair, and he was wearing a uniform of a green shirt, tie, shorts and knee-high socks. When he heard my American accent, he announced that he had just given in his notice that day and was travelling to the States in three weeks. He wanted to hitchhike through Yellowstone National Park. I pointed out that he'd be doing it during a snowstorm by the time he got there. This prompted him to utter one of the best pick-up lines I had ever heard. He announced that this was the last run of his day and if I wanted I could come to the 'end of the line' with him and he'd take me out to dinner. He would tell me where to go in New Zealand, and I could tell him where to go in the US. Done!

He took me to a little café on Customs Street called La Cava, where the 19-year-old Topp Twins were singing. Morri was just about the first person I had ever met who didn't drink, so all this took place stone sober. Later that night, he introduced me to his ex-girlfriend and her new boyfriend, and she rented me a room in her house for $15 a week. Not only was she a fellow American, but we had both been born in Minnesota.

Morri still had a car, so he started taking me on day trips around town, and we eventually decided to travel together. We spent six months hitchhiking around New Zealand, three months picking apples in Australia, and then travelled back to America and racked up 33 states in an old Ford LTD station wagon. On my thirtieth birthday, we both permed our hair, got married and bought a house! (I like to say that I was snatched from the jaws of spinsterhood at the eleventh hour.) I made a snap decision to live permanently in New Zealand, and I have never regretted that decision.

Mary says the Sky Tower now stands on the corner where she and Morri first met — a monument, she feels, to their love and its power.

*

When you know, you know. Even when you don't know who those other guys are …

> *In 1972, I boarded a bus at Porirua arranged by a local radio station, to travel to Auckland to see Joe Cocker at Western Springs Stadium. I was a long-haired teenager. At Paekakariki the bus stopped to pick up three people — two guys and a beautiful girl. I assumed one of the guys to be her boyfriend but, despite that, decided I was going to marry that apparition.*
>
> *On the way back (being a cocky teenager), I managed to squirrel into a seat beside her, weaving my charms and establishing that one of the guys was her brother, the other a mate of his.*
>
> *We were married three years later. We did our big OE together as hubby and wife, lived in Aussie for eight years, returning with two young 'Aussies'. We were 13 years married before we had our kids, so we*

are relatively old compared to some of their mates' parents, but both are great boys, and one has given us four grandkids with another on the way. The other is in Aussie with his lovely partner.

We recently celebrated 40 years married, and I still love her to pieces.

— Graham Ward

*

It's mid-1979 and Rosalene gets a puncture on Ngāmotu Road in New Plymouth. A young bloke — 'nice enough' she says — kindly stops to help her. Graham recognises her because she's the new PR person who started with the company the week before but, because she'd met everyone at the job in a great rush, Rosalene doesn't remember having met him before at all.

Later that morning, without mentioning the roadside rescue, Graham bets the blokes at work a couple of bottles of beer that he can get the new girl, Rosalene, to go out with him. He just fails to mention that he's *already* asked her to the upcoming work do, and she's *already* said yes — she says it would have been impossible to refuse her knight in shining armour. Obviously, Graham wins the bet with his mates. We like Graham.

Cars continued to play a role in their blossoming romance — this was during the era of Prime Minister Rob Muldoon's 'carless days', a quaint little Kiwi exercise in reducing petrol consumption during the late-1970s oil crisis after the revolution in Iran. Every car in New Zealand was stickered with the name of a day, and you couldn't drive it on that day of the week. The aim was to force people to carpool and thereby reduce petrol consumption. It was unpopular and largely ineffective (counterfeiters did a roaring trade in fake exemption stickers), but it worked a treat for Rosalene and Graham.

> *Graham had a 'Wednesday' carless day sticker on his old banger, and I had a 'Tuesday' carless day sticker on my cute wee bright yellow Bambina, so we took each other backwards and forwards to work for the next few months. Cheers, Rob Muldoon.*
>
> — **Rosalene and Graham Bradbury**, Ruakaka

*

Even the simplest stories can come with a little sprinkling of magic dust. Garyth and Sandy Helg live in Australia these days — he sells cars, she sells car parts, which is already sweet — but back in 1994 they were living in Auckland. In fact, it turns out they'd met a long time before that, although they didn't know this until they'd been married for 14 years.

I met my wife, Sandy, at a bar in Manukau City in February 1994. I had met Sandy's sister the week before, and she arranged a blind date for the following week. Sandy is five years older than me. We hit it off straight away, and in March 1994 we were engaged. In October 1994 we were married in a backyard wedding (sister's place). We are still happily married to this day.

A little twist … When I was 15 years old, I used to work on a milk run around the One Tree Hill area, and three or four times a week we approached a house for delivery and my boss would always tell me to take a bottle of orange juice to the 'hot, pretty girl' who was waiting at the top of the driveway. I did this every week for over eight months.

Before we moved to Australia seven years ago, we went for a drive around the old area and I was pointing out different places. When we got to this particular street, I mentioned that I did the milk delivery around that area. My wife asked if I remembered a blonde girl at the top of the drive who was waiting for her milk and was always given a bottle of orange juice … You guessed

> *it! That was my future wife! Turns out she married her milk boy.*
>
> *I saw my old boss a few days later and reminded him about that girl he fancied. He was stunned to learn that I married her.*
>
> — **Garyth (and Sandy) Helg**, Australia

*

And there's something about the milkman, right? I'm not wanting to add here to the 'lusty milkman' myth — just maybe saying that if you have a milk run as a kid and visit a lot of addresses, there's a chance that sometime later you might end up married to one of your old customers. These days, Mike is a truck driver (not milk) and Claire is a volunteer. And it wasn't exactly love at first sight …

> *My wife and I met in 1981 — she was 16, I was 19. We both thought the other looked like a dick. We started going out, though, as 'office' romances develop like that sometimes, and were on and off for many years. We went to England and came back pregnant, and I saw my daughter born. When Jess was 18 months old, Claire and I split for four years and we both matured, so in*

1998 I proposed. Jess was our flower girl — she was 10 years old.

The funny thing is I delivered milk to Claire's place when I was 10 years old. And in the Sixth Form my best friend was her neighbour. Perhaps it was Fate.

— **Mike Howell**, Mt Roskill, Auckland

*

It's not just kebabs or pizza or milk that get the party started. Sometimes all it takes is a gourmet picnic of the finest charcuterie, delicate pastries and soft smoked cheese, a spectacular view of New Zealand's highest mountain, and a splash of NV champagne chilled naturally in a stream fed by glacial waters. This is how Chris Larking did his wooing on the side of Aoraki/Mt Cook.

My beautiful wife, Julie, and I met in the early months of 1992 in a very romantic setting at the Mt Cook Hermitage in the stunning Mt Cook National Park.

Julie had just come back from working in Japan for a few years as an English teacher, having studied Japanese at Avonside Girls' High School and for one year at Christchurch Polytechnic. Julie could speak

Japanese fluently, and was offered the position of Japanese speaker at the very busy Mt Cook Hermitage Travel Desk. Julie was able to welcome Japanese tour groups into the hotel and assist them with booking ski-plane flights, high-country 4WD tours, etc.

My role in the hotel was the resident pianist. I had just finished my Music Degree in Performance Piano (Classical) at Canterbury University, and was looking for some quick cash! I played jazz standards and light pop tunes in the Snowline Bar, which had a stunning view of Mt Cook, from 6pm to 10pm every night, and had a great time entertaining guests from all corners of the world.

Julie's shift didn't finish until 6.30pm so I was able to serenade her with my music across the lobby, and eventually she fell for my melodies — haha!

For our first 'date', the executive chef was gracious enough to make up a gourmet picnic lunch with the finest, tastiest ingredients available. Italian pressed sandwiches with sliced meats and provolone, farm fried chicken pieces with dipping sauces, herbed potato salad with bacon bits, seared venison medallions, fresh local salmon sushi rolls (a Japanese touch!), plus an assortment of pastries and caramel creams for dessert.

On a clear, blue day, windless and serene (only for the occasional rumbling of the Mueller Glacier 800 metres above us), we hiked for about 30 minutes up the Black Birch stream (about 3 kilometres east of Mt Cook Village) until we reached a vantage point that was private and had an amazing view of Mt Cook National Park.

I had also brought along two bottles of Nautilus Cuvée Marlborough Brut NV, which I chilled by wedging them in between rocks in the glacial stream that had made its way down from the Mueller Glacier. Bubbles cooled by Nature … nothing like it!

Absolute perfection and never to be forgotten. (No mobile phones back in the day, so just our own memories have to suffice!)

We had never as much as held hands until that day in April 1992, but after that picnic, we have been together ever since! We were married in Fiji in 1996, and honeymooned in Hawaii the following year. We have two awesome teenage boys who make us very proud.

All thanks to the world's most incredible setting, a glacial stream and a couple of bottles of New Zealand's finest!

— **Chris Larking**, Auckland

*

So there's a taste — a degustation, if you will — of the places people find love. On a bus, on the side of a road or a mountain, in an office or in Antarctica, on the banks of a river, over the garden fence, or in a kitchen at parties. Which doesn't mean, of course, that if you are looking for love you should pick one of those places, go there and wait. That would be silly. And not every story of how couples meet is as uncomplicated as drawing the short straw with a bunch of other nurses who know that doctors, as a rule, make terrible patients, but he turns out to be The One. Sometimes it can be *really* complicated. But these little stories give us a sense of 'Crikey, what were the chances they'd ever meet?', as well as 'That's a terrific way to explain how you began!', and help us make a picture in our head of the kind of people they are. I've never met Alasdair from the medieval re-enactment group, or Graham from the Joe Cocker gig, or Richard from the Oxford–Cambridge Boat Race, but I can imagine a whole life for each of them based on these pivotal moments in their lives.

These elevator-pitch stories were delightful, but what I really wanted to do was re-create the experience I'd had with Ian and Clare over dinner — not just hearing the story, but seeing how they tell it *together.* So I picked a few favourites, tracked people down, went visiting kitchens and living rooms and hotel foyers and sunny gardens and a house-bus, drank cups of tea and ate cake, and sat across from people with my tiny recorder and asked 'So how did you two meet?', then let them tell me. There was a lot of laughter, a bit of arguing, the odd revelation, much talking over one another, and a fair amount of saying exactly the same thing at the same time. Some of the couples were in their thirties, the oldest were in their eighties, and the stories go back as far as the 1930s. The couple who had been together the longest — almost 62 years — were my parents, and it was the first time I'd heard the full story of how they met. But that comes later.

CHAPTER 6

Holding Hands in the Sandpit

BELYNDA SMITH IS A CHILDREN'S LIBRARIAN and has published a couple of books for young readers. **Martin Smith** is a civil engineer. Both were born in Christchurch in 1960. They fell in love at high school, moved in together when they were 17, and married at 19.

More than 40 years later (and still only in their fifties), they have four grown-up children and a grandson. Belynda is a quilter, and some of her work is delightfully Disney-themed. Martin loves his vegetable garden. These days they live in Auckland with their ridiculously cute Cairn terrier, Gretel — named for the character their youngest child played in *The Sound of Music* when she was five. They adore their kids, and it's mutual. I swear that if you wanted to create a New Zealand family sitcom, you would point at these two and say, 'Base it on them!' Remember *That '70s Show*? Belynda and Martin are Kitty and Red Forman, but with the 'ditzy' dialled down. They're playful, but they've also been through some stuff.

There used to be a photograph of them together, aged four, but it was lost in the 2011 Christchurch earthquake. The picture was taken at Kendal Kindergarten in 1964. They were in the sandpit, holding hands.

Martin: We tell people we met at kindergarten, and then had time apart, and then got together again. That's kind of it.

Belynda: We had 13 years apart. [*laughs*]

Martin: [*laughs*] Yeah. That's right.

Belynda: Four till 17.

Martin: That's right.

Me: To explore other options?

Martin: That's right.

Belynda: That's right. [*both laugh*]

It's 1977 and Belynda is a student at Papanui High School, and Martin is at Christchurch Boys' High. She is 17 years old and — it takes us a while to nail this down — Martin is 16.

'I'm pretty sure I was 17,' he says. 'No,' Belynda explains, 'it was August. You were 16 and I was 17. You turned 17 a fortnight later.' Martin agrees cheerfully, 'There we go.'

Belynda's cousin, Steven, was in Martin's class at Boys' High. Steven was also going out with Belynda's best friend, Rose. Although Belynda's and Martin's paths had yet to cross, they'd heard about each other — from Steven and Rose, and other mutual friends. More than one person had said to Belynda 'I think you'd get on really well with Martin Smith.' Steven had also recommended her to Martin.

And then one night Rose wanted to go around to Steven's house, but her mother said she wasn't allowed unless there was somebody else there. Belynda was enlisted to chaperone Rose, and Martin came over to be Steven's wingman. Whether or not it was intended as a blind date, the effect was the same. Rose and Steven broke up a week later; Belynda and Martin have been together ever since.

I ask if there was a lightning-bolt moment when they first saw each other. 'I certainly thought, "Yes!",' Martin says, '"There's something I'd like to see more of."' And then adds, in the way a 16-year-old boy might say it, 'Literally.'

And from Belynda: 'Yes, and I remember Rose rang up the next day, and said, "He really liked you." And I said, "Did he?" And she said, "What did you think?" And I said, "Oh, I liked him, too."' And recalling that conversation now, Belynda giggles exactly as a 17-year-old would.

Martin can picture what Belynda was wearing: cork platform shoes, and dungarees which he didn't entirely approve of because they were difficult to navigate in a dating situation. Defending her modesty, Belynda points out he didn't find that out until later on in their relationship, and then there's some laughter that can only be described as dirty. We all agree that, in any case, dungarees were very much on-trend at the time. 'She was a bit of all right,' he says. 'She's still a bit of all right.'

Belynda: I remember feeling really comfortable with Martin. And safe.
Martin: I remember she was late. I was there first, waiting on the couch. Then she walked in the door.
Belynda: You're only angry about that because you were excited.
Martin: That's right. No, it wasn't anger. It was more … anticipation.

I say how remarkable it is that your first relationship ends up being your only one, before Belynda admits to having had one boyfriend before Martin. Coincidentally (New Zealand is a very small country), I briefly dated the same boy a decade or so later. 'Well, we've all made *that* mistake,' I joke. Martin laughs like a drain. 'Are you going to put that in? You should. That's funny.' They're still friends (well, maybe only until the ex reads this) but I like the idea that, even after 40 years together, you might laugh quite hard at the expense of your partner's one and only ex.

Aged 17, Martin and Belynda moved into a tiny flat together — a fairly radical move for 1977. Martin remembers this as being 'exciting' and 'adventurous'. Did he enjoy the sense of rebellion? 'No, I enjoyed the company.' He was at Canterbury University studying engineering, and Belynda supported them both by working at the public library.

They lived on the smell of an oily rag — Belynda's annual salary was $4000. For her birthday one year she asked her parents if they'd give her a pair of shoes. Her father said, 'Oh, well, we sponsored the refugees at the church, so yes, we can probably sponsor you for a pair of shoes.' It took her father a long time to come to terms with the idea that they'd moved in together — although Martin didn't pick up on the disapproval as much. He was just excited to have her so nearby.

But they both remember the wider social disapproval towards two teenagers 'living in sin' in the 1970s. Belynda had always been involved in Girl Guides and Rangers, but when she and Martin got together she joined Venturer Scouts instead, because that's where Martin and all their mutual friends were. They both studied for and passed their Queen's Scout Award —

the highest honour you can achieve. Martin was presented with his, but when they found out he and Belynda were living together, she wasn't allowed hers — her moral standards weren't high enough.

Me: But yours were okay?
Martin: Too right. Yes, I know. Double standards! Fantastic! That's a fact, too; it really is. There's a letter somewhere that says that.

Belynda appealed against the decision, but they refused to budge. She was, they said, leading Martin astray. It still rankles a bit. Not so long ago, Martin was National Chairman of the New Zealand Scouts Association, and Belynda suggested, not entirely joking, that he could use his position of power to give her the award retrospectively, but apparently that's not how it works. There's a fair bit of joshing about this — in both directions. Belynda says she still has hope they will award it posthumously.

He may not have been able to wangle her a Queen's Scout Award, but Martin would cheerfully give her a medal for putting him through university while working and also studying for her library qualifications. That meant she'd spend six weeks at a time in Wellington, and they both hated being apart. He'd make her bran biscuits and send them to her when she was away. 'So romantic!' Belynda teases — in reference to the bran rather than the gesture — but he says it *was* romantic. 'You forget these things with time, don't you? Sometimes you've just got to stop and reflect.'

They weren't in any rush to get married, although they knew they would eventually. And then one day Belynda couldn't work out why they were waiting. So two years and three months after turning up after school to play chaperone for their friends, Martin and Belynda tied the knot. They were 19.

There was a proposal on the banks of the Avon, Belynda says, at which point Martin blurts, 'Oh, that's right, yes!' 'What do you mean, "that's right"?!' she says, all mock-horror that he might have forgotten this moment. He says he hasn't thought about it for a long time, but when she prompts him with 'Outside the boatsheds', suddenly Martin is throwing in more details about time and place and how it all unfolded. He hasn't really forgotten anything — he recalls the name of the coffee shop opposite the boatsheds, the engagement ring from Stewart Dawson's — 'Still paying it off,' he says. 'It was about $80, wasn't it?' Belynda says. 'Yes!' and they both laugh — and then he's on to the wedding. They had the reception at Bishopdale tennis club, the Girl Guides did the catering, and everyone went to the Bishopdale Tavern while the bride and groom had their photos taken outside Sanitarium. As he pulls each memory out, Belynda affirms them with 'That's right!' and 'Yes!', like he's a gospel preacher and she's giving him a 'Hell, yeah!'.

The road to the altar was rocky, in the sense that they had some trouble finding an altar — or someone to officiate in front of one. The minister at Belynda's parents' Presbyterian church refused to marry them because they were living together (which is all a bit bloody Catch-22, to be honest) so they approached St Giles Church where her parents had been before, but the minister there wouldn't marry them either. Eventually, they found a female minister associated with the church who agreed to do it.

Martin: What was her name? Miss ... ?

Belynda: Miss Biggs.

Martin: Biggs. She had large feet.

Belynda: Don't say that.

Martin: Why not? There's a photo. I took a photo, so I could show you. If we've still got it.

Me: [*Fails to ask to see the photo*]

Because they were both under 20, they also had to get their parents to sign legal documents granting permission for them to get married. By this point, Belynda's parents were entirely on board — the couple had her parents' blessing as well as their signatures. 'I think it helped that they really liked Martin. If he'd been "an undesirable" it probably wouldn't have helped, but they've always adored him.'

Pretty soon, the couple's relative youth became a source of family humour. Belynda reached the (then) legal drinking age of 20 years before Martin — which meant he could go to the pub at 19, but only if she took him. So her dad would tease them with 'Has Belynda taken you out lately?' and Martin would do a whole sad-face she-never-takes-me-out routine ('We couldn't afford it!' she interjects) and complain that he would have to start making his own homebrew. At which point Belynda's dad would take his underage son-in-law to the pub for a proper beer.

Looking back on all this now, they think the short journey from going-around-together to being a married couple had something to do with the early death of Martin's mother. She had cancer, and died just before they met. Belynda's theory is that if his mother had been alive, Martin might have stayed at home when he went to university and they wouldn't have moved in together. I ask whether losing his mother had accelerated his desire to make a new home and family, and Martin thinks about this for a while and then says, slowly, 'Yes. Yes … I think so. Yes.'

They certainly don't feel like they missed out on anything — there's no hankering for a different kind of wild youth. The only thing they're sorry about is that they didn't meet even sooner so that Belynda could have got to know her mother-in-law. Once, early on, when her father was dropping Belynda off at Martin's place, he mentioned that a lovely woman called Pauline Smith had lived in the same street. And then he asked Martin's last name, and they put two-and-two together. Pauline and Belynda's dad had both served on a Scout committee. He remembered, too, that Martin had won a scholarship to Australia when he was 12, and how excited his mother had been about it when he ran into her in the local supermarket. Belynda is grateful for that connection between their families.

Marrying your childhood sweetheart might be rare in the wider world, but, crikey, it now runs in the Smith family — the three eldest of their four children have done exactly that. Belynda runs down the list: 'Thomas and Erin met at high school; Sam and Meg met at university; Kate met Dave at 14.' Martin chips in: 'They met at a Scout jamboree in Christchurch.' 'Bloody Scouts,' I say. 'I know,' he laughs. 'If someone tells you to tie knots, you think again! What happens under canvas ...' Much laughter all round.

This phenomenon is not, they say, the result of any kind of expectations they have for their kids, it's just that they grew up seeing that it works as an option. Same for the children of their friends: if a parent says, 'You're too young to know if they're the right person!', their kids will point at Mr and Mrs Smith and say, 'But it worked for them!'.

So what does make it work for them? 'Trust. And kindness,' Belynda says. 'I think probably Martin is one of the kindest people I know. And I see that in our children as well.' And Martin adds, 'Good company. Going through the good times, the bad times ...' Then, in a really calm way, the pair talk about the challenges they've faced. Belynda was diagnosed with cervical cancer when their youngest child was born. They were living in London at the time, coping with four very young children as well as Belynda's diagnosis and treatment. Before that, one of their sons had life-threatening asthma attacks, and now another son is dealing with serious health issues. They're full of praise and respect for how he and his wife are dealing with it, and the way all of the siblings take care of each other.

They are a tightknit bunch, possibly because the family moved around so much with Martin's engineering work. They were in London for seven years, and bounced around New Zealand at various times — Christchurch, Hamilton, Dunedin, Christchurch again, London, Nelson, Auckland, back to Christchurch, and now in Auckland once more. But no matter where they've lived, they both say, the kids have always had each other. They have their own Facebook group called 'The Smith Set', and if someone puts something on there, no matter whether it's Thomas in Australia or Kate in London, all of a sudden there's a whole ripple of comments. They keep an eye on each other.

The Smith Set take holidays together, and make sure they make a fuss of birthdays, Father's Day, Mother's Day and Christmas. Son Sam writes an annual family Christmas song. 'He starts about October, and does all this build-up to it, and then we all wait with bated breath for the family song to come out, and he incorporates everyone in it,' Belynda explains. 'The chorus is always, "You can't have Christmas without Sam. He's wonderful, he's marvellous, the human embodiment of the human race" or something.' 'Human spirit,' Martin says, helpfully. Fair enough, I say, if you're the one writing the song it might as well be about you. Quite right, they both agree.

And then there's the family chocolate pudding recipe that no one is allowed until they're actually married — living together isn't enough; Martin won't let them have it until the knot is officially tied. On Sam and Meg's wedding day, Meg's first question after the ceremony was, 'When do I get the recipe?' As a father of four, Martin reckons it's good to have a trump card up your sleeve.

I ask whether there is a danger, after all these years as a couple, that they could take each other for granted. Belynda says she's proud of Martin — what he does, what he's achieved and who he is. She thinks they're very lucky, but is still mindful that it would be easy to become complacent. 'It would be easy to think, "We've got it right, we don't have to work at it."' If things aren't going well, does someone call a meeting? 'We don't call a meeting *per se*,' Martin says, 'but usually at some point there's ... a discussion,' and they both burst into laughter.

What *has* changed over the years is 'letting stuff go'. Belynda says she no longer gets bothered quite so much about small irritations — like Queen's Scout Awards. Plus some old irritations have been turned into family jokes — even if Martin can't quite remember the original crime. Like the time he arrived down in Christchurch for Belynda's father's funeral with cucumbers.

Belynda: Martin's a really keen vegie gardener, and he didn't want to miss out on pickling the cucumbers. So he arrived on the day of the funeral with a bag of cut cucumbers to pickle.

Me: [*aghast*] You brought the cucumbers from Auckland?

Belynda: To Christchurch. To pickle them. Yes, it was a fairly low moment.

Martin: I don't even remember that.

Belynda: [*warm but firm*] I do.

Martin: [*already knowing he's losing*] Well, it's important. You know, you put a lot of time into a vegetable garden ... [*grasping at straws*] Your father would have been pleased about it.

Belynda: No, he wouldn't. [*laughter all round*] You know what pickling stuff smells like? Imagine if he'd pickled them at my mother's house?

Martin: At times like that you need to keep yourself busy, though, don't you? Idle hands ... I can't remember the saying now, but idle hands aren't good, are they?

Me: No, the Devil will make work for them.

Martin: There you go, see? You know it.

Belynda: Needless to say, they didn't get pickled. They're in the compost bin in Christchurch.

Martin: Did I not bottle them in the end?

Belynda: No, no way.

Martin: I don't remember it.

Me: Of course not. Why would you remember that? You, with your vinegar and your sugar on the day of the funeral.

Martin: Michèle, I thank you for your support ... [*possibly remembering it all too clearly now*] I haven't grown any cucumbers since, I know that. [*all three dissolve into laughter*]

For Martin, the change over the years has been consciously spending less time away from the family. Work took him to places like Hong Kong, Milan and Singapore for three or four weeks at a time, but often projects would be extended even longer. He missed a lot of birthdays. Once, one of the children left a newspaper article about being a workaholic under his pillow. Ouch. The last overseas posting was to Milan one October — supposedly for a month — but he ended up catching the last flight home to his family on Christmas Eve. He decided that was enough, he wasn't going to do it anymore. Every so often the kids remind him that he used to miss their birthdays — and there's nothing he can say to push back on it because, he says, they're right.

Mr and Mrs Smith say they don't really do traditional 'romance' — Martin gets bad hayfever, so Belynda doesn't get flowers, for example. But then they go on to tell one hell of a romantic story. For them, it's the things they do for each other, and the staying in touch. Even if the morning is mad, and they're racing off to do different things, and are tied up during the day, Martin makes a point of grabbing a moment to phone Belynda — and just thinking about hearing his familiar voice on the phone at random times makes Belynda trail off into a sigh.

Martin explains they've got 'Find Friends' now on their mobiles so they can track each other with GPS at any time — which initially sounds a tad creepy, until I remember they were living in Christchurch on the day of the February 2011 quake. They couldn't find each other for several hours, which Martin, in his wildly understated way, describes as 'a bit of a worry'. He had gone around to their apartment block to see whether she was there, because he didn't know what she was doing that day. She wasn't there. 'I think maybe the car wasn't there,' he says, 'so I knew that you weren't there, but then I didn't know for a couple of hours that she was okay. Or where she was. I had no idea where she was. That wasn't very good.'

There was a message on the answer-phone that Belynda kept for ages. It said: 'Polly, it's Dad here. I'm all right but I can't find Mum. If you hear anything, please let me know.' Every time she played it, it made Belynda gasp.

'Martin was allowed into our apartment to dig through the rubble and try to find me. He knew we would probably never be allowed back in again, because it was so damaged. He got my slippers, my curling tongs, my Birthday Book and my makeup purse. So, when we met up again hours later, here were my things.'

And there's a tiny pause while we imagine what Martin must have been feeling in those minutes, and how he would have been thinking hard about the things Belynda would most want — the things that made her look and feel good, her record of dates for important celebrations. Scrabbling through the ruins of their home, looking with her eyes, and still not knowing whether she was safe. And then he adds to the list of rescued items.

Martin: And my cotton buds.

Belynda: And his cotton buds.

Me: Well, yes ... There was a lot of dust flying around, he needed to take carc of that.

Martin: Thank you.

And then Belynda brings it back.

Belynda: I think even *that*, you know ... We might not do romantic things, but *they're* the things that mean so much to me. That even amongst all this and the building rattling and everything, he still thought about what was really important ... Just feeling safe.

> There's a bit to feeling safe with someone, and cared
> for and nurtured.

And I find, listening to them, I seem to have a little something in my eyes. Must have been all this talk of dust.

CHAPTER 7

The Fates versus Maria and Patrick

MARIA MAJSA IS A WRITER, **Patrick Reynolds** is a photographer. Words and pictures. She writes lyrical essays about music and places and moments in time, and where those things intersect, and has also written scripts for *Shortland Street*. He photographs buildings, and urban and natural landscapes, and tutors in architecture at Auckland University. They met in 1989, but should have met many times before that — the Fates tried to introduce them (and so did their friends) for years, at home and abroad, doing their best to ram them together, but it was always 'nearly, but not quite'.

Patrick looks like a chipper Nick Cave, and his voice on my interview tape sounds a touch Alan Rickman (*Truly, Madly, Deeply* rather than Professor Snape). Other people make a Morrissey comparison, and Maria has always been a massive fan of The Smiths, so that works, too. Either way, think brooding good looks, but he chats way more easily and laughs more often than any of that suggests. Maria is one of those long-limbed, effortlessly elegant women who my mother would say could 'wear a sack and still look chic'. She doesn't wear sacks, of course — there's a photo of her, illustrating a piece she wrote on the romance of bicycles, looking stunning in a simple summer dress. On the day we meet, she is classically stylish in jeans. All of this could be intimidating, except they're both so relaxed and interesting and interested, you forget to feel short and ordinary by comparison, and just enjoy watching them both talk.

We meet at their place — a villa that has been thoughtfully redesigned — and pass through the sunny, open kitchen and settle into a kind of womb-like lounging area at the back, with big couches arranged for conversation. The architecture of the conversation is thoughtful, too — listening back to the tape, I can hear how they both begin sentences two, even three times, to say what they really mean. Sometimes they finish each other's sentences; sometimes neither finish a sentence, because they both know where they were going anyway. Several times they laugh so hard they can hardly speak.

Patrick says he likes to start their story like this: 'It's an oversimplification, but I like to say that we met because Maria was my flatmate's girlfriend.' And it's true that at the time that's where they *thought* their story began. But it didn't. It took them years to unravel this: the bars, the mutual friends, the matchmaking ignored. And a fair bit, too, to put it together, including a near-drowning and a diamond ring in a biscuit tin.

So let's watch their story unfold the way the Fates — those white-robed incarnations of Destiny as imagined by the Greeks — would have seen it from above. Feel free to shout 'Oh, *come on*!' and 'How did you miss *that*?' and 'You're *kidding* me!' at appropriate junctures.

Both born in 1962, Maria and Patrick grew up in neighbouring Auckland suburbs — Pakuranga and Howick, respectively. Different schools, but basically next door to each other. Maria says the first time they experienced this thing of 'almost sharing the space, but not quite touching' was in the early 1980s. Patrick's brother, John, ran a café called John's Diner on Albert Street, and Patrick and another brother, Jeremy, worked there all the time — it's how Patrick put himself through art school. It was, Maria remembers, a really cool place to hang out — John made eccentric food and there was a great jukebox. Arty types mixed with *Herald* proofreaders and Datacom nerds.

It was also just a couple of blocks from the hugely popular A Certain Bar, run by Mark Phillips and Peter Urlich. 'Basically,'

Maria says, 'I spent most of my life there, Thursday, Friday, Saturday nights.' Licensed bars kept shorter hours back then, so relatively early in the evening the doors would open and everyone would be vomited out and wander along to John's Diner which was the next stop, and hang out, have coffee, talk and find out where the parties were.

'My friends and I would always wash up there, lured in by the Chocolate Revenge, which was this legendary dessert that John invented, which was— Oh, my God! I saw him make it once, and it was almost toxic waste, it was made of so much dark chocolate and butter. My friends and I used to go in there and have coffees, and eat this chocolate brownie.'

Patrick would have been there — not just in the kitchen, but also serving. Maria remembers talking to John and Jeremy (who was hard to miss with his blue punk hair, not entirely dissimilar to her own deep red version), but she has no memory of Patrick at all. 'Yet there he was, ghosting along beside me.'

In retrospect, Patrick is pretty sure he remembers seeing Maria there on one of her last nights before she left for London — and the details fit. Maria and her girlfriends, Lee and Lisa, had arrived from A Certain Bar and propped themselves up on barstools by the jukebox. 'We were quite drunk, and we started singing songs.' Also in retrospect, she vaguely remembers him, too — as a grumpy face coming out of the kitchen to give them a stern look. Patrick says that if anyone had told him that night he would end up marrying one of those three women, he would have laughed quite hard. Not because he disapproved of them, just because that would have suggested 'unrealistic expectations' on his part.

So, could have met; probably best they didn't. And then Maria was gone. Needing to escape a violent father, she took off to London and stayed there for years, living in squats, scrabbling around, seeing bands, and working in publishing. Then when Patrick had graduated from art school in 1985, he headed to London, too.

Maria: There we were, both living in London. At some point, I was working for a tiny publishing company in Soho called Aladdin Books. Literally diagonally opposite was a little brasserie called Soho Brasserie where Patrick was a waiter.

Patrick: On the same street, Old Compton Street.

Maria: The same street in London. I used to go for lunch there, and Patrick was working there at the same time.

Patrick: Full-time, all the time.

Maria: Yes.

Patrick: Split shifts.

Maria: He would have been serving lunch and stuff. We possibly walked past each other every day on the way to work, and nothing happened, right? But the Fates were still having a go, though, because …

Patrick: All of this is good, because if we'd met then, I would have fucked it up. The Fates had a plan.

Indeed, the Fates had two serious shots at nudging them closer in London. The first was when Maria happened to be looking out the window of her first-floor office on Old Compton Street and spotted a friend from New Zealand.

'I used to be in a really rubbish band years ago, and our manager was called Steve Heim. I saw him just walking along the street in Soho, and I hadn't seen him for years. It was one of those bizarre out-of-context moments. It's like, "Steve, what are you doing here?"' she laughs. 'I opened the window, and I shouted at him across the street. "Steve!" He was like, "Huh?" We had this shouted conversation. "What are you doing? How long have you been here? We should catch up!"'

Still shouting from the street, Steve explained he was staying with his half-sister, Simone, in St Pancras, and Maria should come over for a drink. She wrote his number down (this is the era of the landline) and promised to call and arrange a time. And meant it — she'd hadn't met Simone yet, and thought it would be fun. But when she tried the number, she discovered she'd written it down incorrectly and whoever answered wasn't Steve. And there was no way to find him again. Which was something of a shame, because the number he'd given her was actually Patrick's — Simone was Patrick's flatmate, and Steve was sleeping on the floor at their flat.

How are we doing, Fates? Frustrated? Little bit, yeah.

The next nudge came a few months later. Still at the same publishing house, Maria worked with a children's book writer and editor, Kate. 'She and her husband were both in publishing, and were always going to launches and openings, and afterwards everyone would repair to this little restaurant called Joe Allen.' Together, Maria and Patrick describe it as the kind of place media people and theatre luvvies liked to frequent. And Patrick would know the clientele pretty well — by now he'd left the Soho Brasserie and was working at Joe Allen.

Using her best received-English voice, Maria does an impression of Kate coming into work one morning and announcing, 'I have found you a man.'

> Maria: She said, 'You have to go to this restaurant.' I was like, 'Oh yeah, whatever.' And she said, 'No, no, no. He's really, really handsome. He's literally tall, and dark, and handsome … I think he might be

from either Australia or New Zealand, because he's got a bit of an accent.'

Patrick: She didn't know she wasn't selling it, though, because that was the last thing you wanted!

Maria: I just wasn't keen, but she was going, 'No, no, no, I think you'd really fancy him. I think he's really your type. He looks a little bit like Morrissey.'

Which, years later, made it abundantly clear to Maria, Patrick *and* Kate that the object of her matchmaking — the sole tall, dark, handsome, possibly-Australian-or-Kiwi Morrissey-doppelganger waitperson at Joc Allen in 1985 — was Patrick. 'There was a guy from Perth,' he says, 'but he was quite obviously gay, so … yes.'

Four shots at it, then: John's Diner, Soho Brasserie, a wrong number and an unsuccessful matchmaker. Still no cigar. Independently (and somewhat reluctantly), they both made their way back to Auckland. Patrick pretty soon threw himself into something intense with someone who he thought was The One. She, however, didn't. He was heartbroken. 'You've got to have your heart broken once, right?' he says now, with inordinate cheer. Maria, meanwhile, struggled to settle back into life at home, and spent a year, she says, feeling lost.

The next time the Fates tried to squeeze them together — a

somewhat convoluted attempt at getting them to meet, it must be said — was when Maria met Patrick's flatmate and started going out with him. This time, Patrick noticed her — he was actually in the room when it began.

Maria: My friend Claire was a journalist, and she invited me to this New Year's Eve party.

Patrick: Which are always the worst parties in the world.

Maria: They're the worst, oh God. Everyone trying desperately to have a good time.

Patrick: And there's no reason—

Maria: No.

Patrick: —other than the arbitrary calendar date.

Maria: And I'm rubbish at parties, anyway. I'm basically an introvert.

Patrick: I remember that night.

Maria: Were you there?

Patrick: Yeah, it was just up the road from here. I remember looking across, and Mark was doing his 'making a move' thing.

Maria: No, that wasn't the first time that I met him.

Patrick: Not the first time? Okay, so the second time. What I remember is your body language, and your body language was like 'No chance, mate'.

They might have slightly different recollections about which party Patrick had witnessed, but they agree on the body-language thing. It's fair to say Maria wasn't smitten, but Mark was persistent. After she ran away from him at the New Year's Eve party, Mark got her phone number from Claire. And wrote it down correctly, bless him.

At this point, we need to introduce Maria's mother. 'You could only really describe her as spooky,' Maria says. 'She always knew shit that you had no idea how she knew. It was gobsmacking.' Her name is Dawn — a delightfully appropriate name for someone who keeps turning up to throw new light on things. Dawn passed away a few years ago, but she remains a recurring character in this story as an excellent earthly ambassador for the Fates.

Mark would phone Maria's house, and Maria would tell her mother to say she was out, that she didn't want to talk to him. 'Then she said to me, "Look, you know, you should just go out with him." I said, "Why? He really isn't my type, Mum, at all." She said, "I know, but sometimes you have to throw yourself into things, and other things happen. You just don't know."'

The next time Mark rang, Dawn handed Maria the phone. Mark was funny and entertaining, and he'd travelled and had good stories. They started seeing each other, though, Maria says, there wasn't very much there. And then she says, as though she's curious about this herself, 'It was an odd thing. I've never done that before. I've never gone out with someone who I didn't really feel a strong pull towards.'

Mark flatted in an old, freezing-cold villa with a lean-to kitchen at the back. The only house rule was that, if you had a guest over, you had to do the cooking. But the kitchen was small and nasty — not big enough for cat-swinging, or for hanging out in with your drink while someone cooked — which meant your guest would be up the hall in the living room with your flatmates. One of whom was Patrick. Mark would be cooking, Patrick would be sitting with Maria at the other end of the house.

There was no dramatic epiphany in the living room — 'You're with the wrong one!' — just a slowly developing friendship over easy chats and shared jokes (out there in the kitchen, Mark had a habit of putting chilli in everything, which amused them both), but always with the understanding that Maria was Mark's girlfriend and therefore out-of-bounds. A very un-Kiwi beginning to a relationship, we all agree — usually we tumble into bed and wake up the next day and say, 'Now, what are you like?' Patrick says it was the first time he'd become friends with a woman before anything else — and it was the best thing ever.

This went on for about six months — still with Maria somewhat bewildered about what she was doing with Mark. 'It was for a reason,' Patrick insists. 'The Fates had to organise this thing. It was a bit of a rumpty machine, but it rumbled along.'

Cue the Fates arranging a second appearance from Maria's mother. Dawn and Maria are having lunch one day in Vulcan Lane when Patrick and his brother John walk in. Introductions all round, followed by a pleasant chat. 'Next time I spoke to my mum, she said, "That Patrick's really nice, isn't he?" I said yeah. She went, "No, he's *really* nice." I went, "What do you mean?" She said, "Well, he's The One. You're with the wrong one. Mark's not the one, *he's* the one." I remember laughing. I was going, "What are you *talking* about, Mum?" Then it was like, "Oh, fuck."'

For Maria, the pieces of the jigsaw suddenly fitted together: this was why she had been hanging out at Mark's — because Patrick was there. But she had no idea what Patrick was thinking. Because Patrick, by his own admission, wasn't thinking anything at that point. 'Simple souls, men,' he says. 'I didn't have a spiritual adviser, you see?'

Next up, the Fates try a little life-and-death scenario. Patrick's family has a beach house at Anawhata on Auckland's wild, woolly west coast. One weekend, Mark told Maria that all three of them were going to hang out at the bach — something they occasionally did. But when they went swimming at White's Beach — Mark encouraging Maria to head out deeper — they were caught in a strong rip. Maria credits Patrick with saving them all (he says he could barely save himself), because he was the one who understood it was a rip they'd been caught in, and that the only way to get to shore is to swim across rather than against the waves. They made it out, but only just. 'I remember literally crawling onto the sand. My muscles were twitching like I'd used every ounce of strength I had to get out. And Patrick was really lovely, and really solicitous. He was like, "Oh, my God, are you okay?"' Mark, meanwhile, did the full, blokey 'Call that a rip? That was nothing!' routine. Maria found that … interesting.

But on the way to telling me this story of nearly drowning — clearly an often-talked-about drama in their shared memories — Patrick and Maria unearthed a new memory from the same day.

> Patrick: [*slow dawning*] I think that was the day [*stops to laugh*] that I saw you in a different light … In the supermarket.
>
> Maria: [*dissolves into laughter*] Yes?!
>
> Patrick: We were getting supplies, right, because you've got to take everything.

Maria: The weird thing was, me too! I don't know if I've ever told you that. I was with Mark, and we had this little trolley, and you had your little basket, and you were walking along. [*both are barely able to speak through the laughter*] The thing is we turned up this aisle, and you were walking towards us.

Patrick: Ooh, back-lit!

Maria: You had your shades on. You were just looking quite ... All of a sudden, it was ... [*makes a noise like a monk chanting*] ... It was like there were rays coming out of him.

There's a pause as we ponder the majesty of this moment in the snack aisle. And then, to lighten it, Patrick adds, 'I can't make it that spiritual — it was your legs. I think you had a short skirt on.'

Next, the Fates up the ante — instead of squeezing them together, they try reverse psychology and pull them apart. Patrick decides to go back to Europe for a six-week holiday and throws a little going-away party. Mark can't come (he's working nights) (shame), but Maria can. She makes Patrick — wait for it — a mix-tape. For younger readers I should explain: recording a bunch of your favourite songs onto a cassette was a classic romantic move. It's not only an intimate expression of your musical tastes, but also an opportunity to pour all kinds of meaning into your track choices. We didn't need Tinder profiles, because we could make mix-tapes. Everyone over 40 has at least one in a shoebox somewhere. Hopefully from the person they're still with. They're that significant.

At the party, Maria gives Patrick the tape done up in wrapping paper with a card. He suggests they go to his room to open it. Smooth move? Not consciously, but at some level he thinks so. He'd had some wine. 'God knows, without alcohol, how these things happen,' he wonders. ('Cheers!' say the Fates.)

Patrick unwraps the gift — it's a really sweet moment. The vibes were irresistible. Patrick knows a formal 'thank you' is insufficient. He launches himself at Maria. She's not quite expecting that. Their teeth clash. It was their first kiss, and it is The Worst Kiss in the World. 'A dental collision,' Patrick calls it. They laughed about it, and nothing else happened. Except there was a chink in the curtain now. (At last!) But just a chink.

Patrick says he'll stay in touch and see what happens when he gets back. Maria knows she's got six weeks to end things with Mark. Her problem, though, is that she doesn't know how to do that. 'I had always been the dumpee. I'm not good at this, and it was such a horrible thing that I didn't want to do it. The weeks kept slipping by, and I hadn't told him.'

Meanwhile, Patrick is sending romantic postcards from London (including Bresson's *The Kiss*, possibly as a template for something to try next time). Maria is writing long letters back. The weeks go by. Five of them. She still can't do the dumping. So the Fates take it out of her hands and give the job to Mark. He makes a vital mistake — the details don't matter — but suddenly it's as clear to him as it is to her that their relationship is over.

A week later, Maria is housesitting for a friend and there's a knock on the door. Her mother has given Patrick the address, and there he is, with gifts from England. 'Morrissey singles, and flowers and things. He just turned up there, and that was kind of … Yeah, then we were together.'

There are a few weeks of climbing in and out of windows — Patrick was still flatting with Mark, and they wanted to be discreet. Eventually, they moved together into brother John's newly bought house. This is 1989. In the early 1990s they went back to England and pieced together all of the near-misses on Old Compton Street. It was, they both agree, 'revelatory'.

One more story, with one more spectacular appearance from Maria's spooky mother. Patrick says he was never one of those people who had always wanted to get married. 'Or even thought about marriage. Or kids. I just — quite suddenly — had this urge to ask Maria to marry me. I couldn't get rid of it. I tried!' he laughs. The idea came completely out of the blue — they'd only just moved in together — and the only person he told about this terrible urge was his brother John. 'I said, "Look, I'm giving myself two weeks to recover from this malady, and if at the end of that I haven't, well, then I'll go with it."'

Before the two weeks are up, he gets a call from Dawn who, apropos of nothing, has this to say: 'By the way, just letting you know there's a family ring. If there was a need for it, there's a great-aunt's diamond ring in the biscuit tin.' The timing, Patrick says, was uncanny. He whipped out to Pakuranga and picked it up.

Under cover of 'just another weekend at the bach', Patrick plots the proposal. He manages to secrete a bottle of champagne, plus ice, plus flutes, into a rather large bag, which was clinking (Maria assumed it was photographic equipment) and suggested they go for a walk. They climbed to the top of the headland between Piha and White's Beach, where it juts out over the roiling surf. Pōhutukawa cling to the cliff, Patrick says, and Maria reckons that when you're up there you feel like you're on the edge of the world. It was a perfect, cloudless day. They sat down under a kowhai tree.

'And then I proposed to you,' Patrick says, '... and you didn't say a thing.' Maria was so surprised by his 'Would you like to spend the rest of your life with me?' that she couldn't speak. And didn't speak for a long time. It suddenly dawned on Patrick that he had forgotten to consider that the answer might be 'no'. Hilarious now, when they tell it — 'Hang on ... This is the point you have to say something!' — but eventually Maria found her voice and said 'yes'. They drank the champagne, ran down to the beach and threw themselves in the ocean. Back at the bach, brother John took engagement photos (there was a camera in a different bag), and a year later — 1992 — they were married up on that same cliff top. They call it Proposition Point. It's this *place* they celebrate rather than dates of meetings, or almost-meetings. They have three children — Rosza, Laszlo and Rainer — and their placentas are buried there, too.

I tell them that, as much as they frustrated the Fates, they actually responded to every opportunity in exactly the right way — it was about timing, wasn't it? Exactly, they both say. The London matchmaking would have been too much pressure for Maria; their friendship was able to blossom because romance was off the table thanks to Mark; and thanks to the woman who had broken his heart, there was a softness and vulnerability to Patrick that year, too.

We talk a bit about the romance of landlines and mix-tapes and postcards.

Patrick: The kids just can't believe how anyone ... How did anyone have sex before the cellphone? That is the agency of connection now.

Me: That's right.

Patrick: I just point out, 'You know, we somehow met each other.'

[*The Fates smile wryly, and take a collective bow.*]

CHAPTER 8

Break-ins, Bruises, Blind Dates and Other Bad Starts

WHAT DID WE LEARN from Patrick and Maria? That at some point the two of you have to just bloody well end up in the same room. Patrick put it pretty succinctly: 'You can only marry someone you've met.' But also, you know what? That meeting doesn't have to be auspicious. Sometimes it's a disaster. It might be hate-at-first-sight, or involve some light breaking-and-entering, or perhaps there's three of you on the blind date, or maybe one of you ends up in A&E.

*

An email lands in my inbox from **John Bannock.** Back in 1987, John had turned up at Wellington's CIT to do a block course in engineering. While he was waiting at the administration desk for the key to his room at the student hostel, he got distracted and misheard his room number. When the key didn't work in the door, he tried to force it, and almost managed to break in before a perfectly lovely young woman opened it from the inside. John was still so convinced he had the right room he almost managed to make **Genevieve** believe that *she* was in the wrong room — despite the fact she'd been living in it for several days, all unpacked and everything. It was resolved by a phone call to the admin desk, and John slunk off to find the right door for his key.

'I spent the next two weeks seeing her at a distance during "O" week, and I was in my room late one Friday night when there was a knock on the door of the dorm — it was Gen. Upon asking what she wanted, she said she was there to see me!'

See? Women are good at finding things. John was 20, Gen was 18. They were married seven years later. Gen is still a tiny bit ticked off, John says, with the timing of his proposal, though, which was (literally) just as she was about to fly out of LA to the UK. 'It was the last day of our USA trip together. I was planning on doing it at the Grand Canyon, but had just read several articles about the number of people who fell off the edge during photos, which I always thought was a bit "Darwin" funny: "Mum — a bit to the left, Granny make way for Tarquin, Dad a bit to the right — bugger, where's Granny now?" And also, we were there with friends.'

He let the Grand Canyon moment pass, and then suddenly he was running out of time. Gen was leaving America for the UK a week earlier than John (she had booked a cheap flight), and he went to see her off. At the last possible minute — in the departure lounge at Tom Bradley airport — he popped the question. She had to come back through Customs clearance to say 'yes'. Their first photos as an engaged couple were taken by a Japanese tourist with a camera. (This is 1993, pre-cellphone, no selfies.) They have never seen the photographs.

Even with John originally from the North Island, and Gen from the South, John says they discovered numerous links between their families, so their wedding in 1994 was something of an extended family reunion. They now live in Governors Bay. Gen still thinks the danger of falling into the Grand Canyon isn't a good enough reason to propose in an airport.

*

A less than fabulous geographic location can be a bonus. At a corporate event on the Gold Coast, I met a woman (let's call her **Cathryn**) who told me she'd met her now-partner at a National Party Conference in Masterton. (Masterton is a pleasant little town, but is rarely referred to as 'the Paris of the Pacific'.) Cathryn firmly believes that if you can fall in love at a gathering of political boffins in a small town during winter — possibly, I'm guessing, involving a motel room with floral curtains and candlewick bedspreads — everywhere you go together after that feels, by comparison, incredibly romantic.

*

Over a business lunch at Te Papa, **Nick Hearn** told me that when he was at university there was a girl he couldn't stand. It was mutual. She smoked and he hated that; she thought he was a prize wanker. No interest in each other whatsoever. Ten years later ('Ten years!' Nick marvels), they bumped into each other through a group of mutual friends at the Rhythm and Vines concert near Gisborne in 2010. 'We hadn't spoken to or seen each other all that time. And it ended up being the happiest summer of my life.' Nick asked **Janine** out for coffee about 19 times during the festival, but she said 'no', until right near the end when she phoned to invite him over to her campsite for a barbecue. His response? 'Only if you have beer.' Which is a big call for a guy who has been turned down for coffee 19 times. She said, 'Yeah, plenty of beer.' Afterwards, she admitted that after this call she'd gone, 'Fuck, I've got to go and get beer!'

Nick works for a power company, Janine is a zookeeper. 'We did everything in reverse,' Nick says. After 18 months together they did their big OE — 23 countries in seven months. 'We saw the best and the worst of each other. I was almost airlifted out of Nepal to Singapore — we were deep in the jungle and I got this weird illness — but they took me to Kathmandu instead. I was out to it for three days, and she was right there beside me the whole time.'

They came home and had their first son, Hunter. 'And then after Hunter came along, I realised that, contrary to my belief of not wanting to get married, I did want to. So I proposed. She didn't say "yes", because she was crying — but I took it as a "yes".' I suggest to Nick that might have just been a post-partum thing — women will cry at anything after giving birth, right? — but he assures me Hunter was about a-year-and-a-half by then. So they got married, and then they had Zac.

Curious about what ends up being important, I ask if she'd still been smoking when they met 10 years on. 'It did come up,' Nick says, 'but ironically at Rhythm and Vines I was having a cheeky durry when I saw her. Bit of a contradiction, yeah.'

*

The Blind Date is a seriously high-risk venture. It's hard to tell which is the most anxiety-inducing — is it the chance you won't like them, or the prospect of them not liking you? Imagine how truly terrifying it was back in 1984 when you couldn't do a little pre-date Facebook-stalking, let alone see a photo of the intended on your matchmaker's phone. Yep, we did hard-core blind dates in The Olden Days.

So there's the obvious stuff to worry about — what should you wear, will they be recognisably human, can you convincingly fake anaphylactic shock if it all goes pear-shaped? Then there's the chance — and you probably haven't even considered this — that he turns up for the blind date *with his girlfriend*.

If you were going to make a movie out of **Soraya and Jim Hogan's** lives thus far, you could reasonably cast Ruby Wax and Billy Connolly in the lead roles (assuming Ruby could pull off a girl from Tauranga and Billy could play an Auckland Westie). Soraya is a feisty dynamo with dark curls; Jim is all salt-and-pepper goatee and sardonic wit. She teaches English as a second language; he's an artist and an auctioneer. They have a son and daughter, born in 1993 and 1996 respectively, who still live at home. Jim and Soraya disagree on almost everything, talk all over each other, and tell entirely different bits of their story at the same time, with neither of them willing to budge. Sometimes it's like *The Muppets'* Statler and Waldorf got married and have spent three decades heckling each other. And then they'll say something so kind and heartfelt about what they mean to each other that it takes your breath away.

So it is typical of them that, even though Jim loves this version of their first meeting and tells it at dinner parties himself, he still argues with Soraya about whether they were actually on a blind date that night or not.

It goes like this. Soraya is new to Auckland — she's finished at Waikato University and has moved to Glenfield to stay with her sister, Angela, to give her and the brother-in-law a bit of a hand with their new baby. The Police are coming to Auckland (not as in *whee-oo, whee-oo* — the band with Sting), and there's nothing Soraya likes better than a live gig. But she doesn't know many people in the Big Smoke and doesn't want to go on her own. Angela suggests she goes with her friend Mary (who Soraya hasn't met yet) and Mary's boyfriend, John. Plus Mary has an old friend from school, Jim, who's keen to see The Police, so he could make up the foursome. There is clearly a bit of nudge-nudge-wink-wink matchmaking going on here, so Soraya says that she'll go with Jim if he buys her ticket.

Jim: [*still outraged*] You'll go if I pay for the ticket — this is how it got back to me.

Soraya: I think I just said that flippantly.

Jim: [*re-enacting the conversation*] 'Will you buy her a ticket?' I said, 'Who? No! Why?!' [*to Soraya*] Continue.

Soraya: Thank you.

Jim: I shall interject at the appropriate times.

Soraya: The night of the concert, Mary picks me up—

Jim: She was driving a little orange Corolla.

Soraya: Yeah, that's not relevant, is it?

Jim: No, but I can remember that car. Unfortunate colour choice for a car.

In the orange Corolla, Soraya gets to know Mary and John as they head over to pick up Jim from work. And there he is, waiting for them with — surprise! — his girlfriend. Bit of squash in the back, although room enough for Soraya to check out The Girlfriend's black jeans and V8 pendant. 'I thought if that's the kind of girl he likes, it's not really me. I'm more student op-shoppy, and she was a real Westie … as was he.' If Jim had a type, she thought, she wasn't it.

Soraya had the kind of skills they admire in West Auckland, though — as they enter the stadium for the gig, all the cans of beer secreted in Jim's pockets are confiscated by security, but Soraya floats through with a bottle of bourbon under one arm and L&P under the other. She's also feeling better — she might have arrived with a carload of people she's just met, but she keeps bumping into mates from university. They sit in a row — John, Mary, Soraya, Jim, The Girlfriend — and pass the bottle along. Recalling this bit of their story, Soraya interrupts Jim before he can interrupt her. 'You're going to say that thing that I do not remember,' and then she whispers to me, 'I don't remember this.' 'I recall,' Jim declares, not in the least perturbed, 'that you said I could have a drink "but don't give your friend any".' This is not something Soraya can imagine saying to anyone, ever. Maybe Jim imagined her thinking it.

Nothing happened that night — no lightning-bolt moment (that comes later), no sense they'd just met someone important. Although later in our conversation I find it fascinating that Jim can picture precisely what Soraya had been wearing to the gig: Jag jeans, a pink corduroy waistcoat and leather jandals. He very much liked the leather jandals. Soraya remembers the specific date without any effort: 28 February 1984. Jim surprises both of us when he reveals he still has his ticket to that gig in a box of treasures downstairs.

Meanwhile, Angela and Mary are still matchmaking. Angela writes Soraya's phone number on Jim's bedroom wall — the 1980s equivalent of putting someone's number in your phone. John and Mary continue to gather them up for gigs — The Mockers at Mainstreet, The Narcs and Herbs on the North Shore. (The movie of their life has an excellent soundtrack.) The Girlfriend is no longer in tow. But they're both in limbo: post-university, Soraya has no idea what she wants to do with her life, and neither does Jim. He's vaguely thinking about going to Israel to live on a kibbutz. At 20 years old, if either of them had any kind of radar, settling down certainly wasn't on it.

The pivotal moment was when Soraya's mother became ill. Jim's father had died the previous November, so he was sensitive to the looming grief of losing a parent. In May, when Soraya was called back to Tauranga to visit her mother, Jim insisted he would drive her there. Soraya is the youngest of six kids, and, as an only child, Jim found her big, loud family a delightful novelty — plus, as a bonus, there was a fantastic little music shop called Luigi's in their Greerton neighbourhood. Soraya asked her mother what she thought of Jim. 'She said: "If you marry anyone as nice as that I'll be happy."' Her mother died in June.

They kept visiting Greerton. Jim tells terrific stories about staying with Soraya's dad, Ray. Ray had been a bushman and a logging contractor, and had his own trucking business. He'd tease Jim about his earring, and shout down the hallway in the morning, 'Are you sleeping in the right bed, boy?', before instructing him to cook up lamb chops in lard for breakfast, with Worcester sauce. 'It was heaven,' Jim says. On Saturday nights, the two men would slip down to the local pub, where Ray suddenly swore like a trooper, had a few jugs, and instructed all the other patrons to go home to their families. Ray always won the meat raffle. Back at the family home,

Soraya's brother Greg would call him 'Jim Bob', and Ray would retort, 'He's Jim *Thruppence*, he's not good enough to be a Jim *Bob*!' Jim realised he was being tested, that the family was putting him through some kind of mysterious approval process. He discovered he loved being part of this big, crazy family, and he and Ray got on like a house on fire.

The lightning-bolt struck in September. Back in Auckland, Jim and Soraya took his mother, Pat, out for her birthday to The Birdcage, the iconic old tavern squeezed between Victoria Park and the motorway. At some point, Pat slips off to the bathroom and, alone at their table, Jim is hit by an overwhelming desire to propose to Soraya. It came completely out of the blue — he still looks shocked and stutters a little as he describes it. 'It was just *pooph*, and I went, "Oh my God. Okay, get a hold of yourself. What are you doing?" This feeling was so strong. I just wanted to say "Marry me." I could think of nothing else. I can still remember sitting at the table almost talking — blah, blah, blah, blah — with this going on in my mind, and trying to figure out what had happened. I couldn't. It was such an intense thing. Where did it come from? I don't know. I'm trying to be rational, and I'm saying, "For God's sake, man, what are you doing?" It was like "No, I want to marry her."'

And then — and this is probably testament to the responsibility an only child feels to his recently widowed mother — he thought, 'Oh, God, it's my mother's birthday. God, how will she react?' It didn't feel right that Pat would come back from the bathroom on her very own birthday and find them engaged, her celebration usurped. 'So he didn't,' Soraya says. 'Your mother would have probably fainted.'

It's an intriguing thing, right? This sudden overwhelming urge to propose, experienced by someone who has had no previous inclination to marry. We heard a similar tale from Patrick Reynolds (he described it as 'a malady'), and you can hear it in Nick Hearn's story, too. Something suddenly irresistible.

Jim is still bewildered by this moment, and wonders whether it was his late father or Soraya's mother whispering in his ear. And though the question wasn't asked that night, he'd made his decision. He proposed to Soraya soon after that — casually, they both say, while lying in bed. And he told her that he had wanted to on The Birdcage night, and that he regretted not doing it then. And then the lovely thing is that Soraya is genuinely glad he didn't propose at his mother's birthday dinner — it would have been weird, she reckons — but she's tickled about the blinding flash of knowing.

They were married in Tauranga the following year by an Anglican minister — a woman who was officiating at her first wedding, which Jim says made the day even more special. Her name was Delphine, and they would visit her and exchange Christmas cards each year until she died. I tell them she would have been chuffed — that I've heard marriage celebrants quietly keep a ledger in their heads of how many people they've married who have stayed married. There are probably bonus points if your very first couple lasts more than three decades.

Each year on their wedding anniversary they light the same candle they lit at their wedding ceremony. They've lost it a couple of times, they both admit, and had to use a substitute, but when I ask to see it now it's easy to find — it had been their anniversary a couple of weeks before, so it's in the dining room. 'It's getting a bit low,' Soraya says, 'so we only light it for a few minutes, because, you know, we might have a few more years to go.' Which is said teasingly, but Soraya also says this: 'He is the most caring, hard-working husband and father I could have wished for.'

Then there's some more robust banter.

Jim: We fight, sometimes about the silliest things—

Soraya: We fight because we're different people.

Me: Fighting's good if you resolve things.

Jim: We haven't resolved last night yet — you haven't apologised.

Soraya: Oh. What happened last night? God, I can't even remember.

Jim: [*good-natured*] That sounds fucking right ... It's silly stuff. We've got very different brains, and my brain works very differently to yours.

Soraya: [*also good-natured*] It does. Mine works properly.

And then, without any prompting, Jim says this: 'I've been very lucky that I met Soraya and she's been my partner through life. I don't say "I love you" much, and I know I'm not a great hugger, but you know that, for me, I'd be nothing without you. You've given me everything that we've got. And that's how I see our marriage. If I lost Soraya, I'd be lost, you know?'

*

There are small echoes of Jim and Soraya's story in another one that arrives by email — third wheels, and a family illness that nudges things along. In a nutshell, **Gavin Schist** met his Danish wife on a beach in Thailand, but let's rewind a bit.

Gavin is from Hokitika and, like all good people from small towns, he had a hankering to see the world. After maxing out a credit card on a round trip from Alaska to Alaska — via New York and New Orleans — Gavin hit London in January 2000 to knuckle down and 'get financial'. In the depths of a miserable English winter, he was working outside on a house extension, which wasn't going well — the building plans were vague at best — so there was much standing around in the cold, and scratching of heads.

Gavin's brother, Dan, phoned to say he had a round-the-world ticket, and why didn't Gavin meet him in Thailand? Gavin explained the whole credit-card scenario, but his brother reminded him that his *new* bank account would have a *new* overdraft, so how much could he get his hands on? The answer — six hundred pounds — was heaps more than Dan had. Gavin booked his flight to Bangkok at lunchtime the next day.

'I travelled as the third wheel with Dan and his irritating Aussie girlfriend. Sometimes I'd go for a walk to give them some space in the evenings.' One night, Gavin came running back — he'd found a beautifully lit temple, never seen anything like it, and Dan — a keen photographer — needed to come and get a shot.

Katie: [*nasal whine*] Nah, Dan, stay heer ... eet's not the one in the book, don't go ...

Gavin: Katie, you've got to see it, just the colours; it's the best I've seen so far.

Katie: Dan, don't go, eet's not the one ya wanted to see, I can't even see eet een tha *Lonely Planet*.

You get the picture. They spent a week heading for the full-moon party at Ko Pha-ngan and, after a long ferry and minibus ride, were dropped off at a beach at something like 3am. Gavin remembers walking past hotels and restaurants with cabins behind, but of course none were open at that hour. 'Then I spotted a hammock, and there was no way I was going past that. I settled in and went to sleep, while Dan tried to get a photo of a rat that was creeping down a rope and sniffing my hair, but wasn't quite brave enough to chance walking across my face.'

The next morning they booked into the cabins behind the hammock. Which is where Gavin met **Tine** (pronounced like the end of 'Christine') from Denmark. Initially she rejected Gavin's advances, but she says now she was just a bit giddy from barbecuing herself in the sun and not quite in the right frame of mind. Gavin ditched Dan and Katie, and he and Tine travelled down through Malaysia together.

Which is where Tine had the first chance in a while to check her emails — three weeks' worth. The first ones told her that her father had suffered a serious heart attack and might not make it; the next ones told her he was doing okay — but where was she?; and the most recent ones were along the lines of 'Tine! Are you still alive?!'

Gavin says it was at this point that they became really close — the rollercoaster of emotions, and maybe the sense that life was a serious thing, and that family mattered. Gavin went to Denmark to join Tine for her cousin's wedding; Tine visited him in London; and she came back with him to New Zealand, where Gavin had a job clearing stoat traps on the Haast range. 'She took it in her stride. I'd stagger back to the bach after a day on the hill and be overwhelmed by the smell of baking or a roast in the oven. I promised her a new pair of fancy leather tramping boots, but she chose some lace-up rubber ones instead. "These should work just fine, shouldn't they?" she asked, not realising they have been the uniform in that part of the world for decades.' Gavin's West Coast mates reckoned he'd found a keeper.

They travelled around New Zealand and Australia, spent a summer in Alaska, then moved into an apartment in Copenhagen. In 2005, their daughter Olivia was born, and a year later they were pregnant with their son, Martin. 'Our apartment was getting smaller,' Gavin says. 'You couldn't open the shower door properly, it would hit the bed.' One evening Tine said, 'I think we should move to New Zealand.' Gavin immediately got up from the couch and started packing up the CDs. They moved to Hokitika in 2007, and their second daughter, Kaya, was born there in 2011. Gavin still likes to tell people that he left Hokitika with a backpack and a credit card, and came back with a wife, two kids and a 20-foot container.

*

The first time **Tim** met **Jane**, he ended up in hospital. Something to do with a car door and a blind date with a Waikato farmer's daughter. Keen to hear more, one early spring day I drove to Karāpiro to meet the Sandbrooks. They live semi-rurally in a sprawling modern bungalow surrounded by plenty of lawn. These days, Jane mostly works at home and Tim is a manager at a dairy company. They're lovely, salt-of-the-earth people. If your car happened to break down on the nearby highway, for example, I could imagine that theirs is the kind of door you'd be pleased you'd knocked on for help — they'd welcome you in, and Jane would make coffee while Tim could be relied upon to do something sensible with your car.

As we sit in their neat-as-a-pin kitchen, Tim tells me about his wild youth. He says he was 18 years old when he was thrown out of Dannevirke. It was 1977 and he and his mates used to drive around town 'in huckery old cars and cause a lot of mayhem'. There were speeding tickets pretty much every day, and frequent arrests. He got lucky once — pulled over for drunk driving, but let off because it was his birthday. Gentler times. Tim worked at the post office, which was handy, because each week when he got his pay-packet, he could walk around the back to the courthouse and hand over the entire contents to cover that week's fines. Eventually, a local detective said, 'Look, how about you just leave town, and start afresh, and we'll forget about pursuing you?' Tim thought that was an excellent idea, so he chucked in his job and headed to Hamilton.

He moved in with an aunt and uncle who were hugely kind, even though, Tim says, he continued being a nuisance. His younger cousin Pete was helpful, too — when Tim told him he was keen to find himself 'a sweet chicky-babe', Pete wangled him the phone number of a good-looking girl in a mate's class at school. Tim phoned her a couple of nights later to ask her out. I tell him I'm impressed with the bravery — cold-calling someone you'd never even met for a date. Jane, who was the 16-year-old who took the call, reckons it wasn't courage. 'It was testosterone!' 'Yeah, and I was stupid as well.' Tim grins. 'I was bulletproof.'

Jane told him she might be going out with her boyfriend that night, but if she said that to put Tim off, it didn't work. He, his cousin Pete and the boy from Jane's class drove straight over to her parents' farm. There was a beautiful old homestead with a big hedge and two gates. Tim pulls up at the first gate and goes around the back of the car to open it, but the mate calls out that it's the wrong gate — they want the one further up. As Tim runs back, Pete opens his car door. 'And my foot came up and just caught the corner of the door and instantly duck-egged. I couldn't stand on it. By then Jane had heard us pull up, and she'd come out. I saw her and took a few stumbles, and I was cursing, swearing ... So I grabbed hold of her, and she put her arm around me. I thought, "Oh, this is nice." That was about it. And then I said, "I've got to go to the hospital," so ... off we went to the hospital.'

Jane's dad wouldn't let her go to the hospital with Tim, because she already had a boyfriend and that would have been inappropriate. Doubtless, Dad could see what was already going on between them. 'Love is chemicals,' Jane says. 'You meet someone, and, yeah, it's just chemicals. You just know straight away.' Tim was blindsided. Already a man-of-the-world — he'd had at least 10 girlfriends by this point, he reckons — he knew this was different. 'This was just *bang*! It was bizarre. It was seriously something.'

Less serious was the injury — Tim's duck-egg bruise was diagnosed at the hospital as a burst vein — so he was back on his feet and back on the phone the next day, asking Jane out for a proper date. Despite being deeply unimpressed with his old banger of a car — a 1953 Austin A40 Somerset which he'd nicknamed 'the Austang' (like a Mustang but not, geddit?) — Jane was keen enough to overlook that and go out with him anyway. They headed into town to see some mates, listen to rock'n'roll and drink beer. On the way, Tim made the classic move — rolled the car to a stop, pretending it had broken down — and used it as an opportunity for a pash. Jane wasn't fooled for a second, but quite liked the pash. They were together forever after that.

Both of them say that they sensed in the first few seconds of meeting that they were the right people for each other and that, certainly by the next day, it was definite. Jane asks whether I've seen the kids' movie *Hotel Transylvania*. I haven't, so she explains there's a song in it about how you've got to have 'zing'. 'We had that zing,' she says. 'Yeah. It was amazing.'

She describes Tim as 'a goal-seeker, a big-picture person' who decides what he wants and then goes for it, which meant things moved along pretty quickly after that. 'I've got a letter somewhere that I wrote to him in typing class. That was two weeks after we met, and he was already talking children and marriage and all the rest of it.'

Which wasn't the kind of talk Jane's parents wanted to hear. Jane is the oldest of six kids, and there were expectations that she'd go into nursing (her mum was a midwife), and she was supposed to be doing University Entrance that year. It went badly — 'too many distractions' — and when Tim moved to Palmerston North, Jane left school and went to live with him. The 'leaving home' scene was dramatic, not only because Jane's mother was weeping as they drove away, but also because just down the road the car broke down. Not a fake breakdown for pashing purposes. A wheel actually fell off.

> Jane: I'd finished school and it was like 'okay'. I loaded up my little suitcase and put it in the car, and we got about 3 miles down the road, and the wheel fell off outside the Hautapu dairy factory.
>
> Tim: It just went sideways and smashed the diff' and the brakes all flew off. We couldn't even find the wheel.
>
> Jane: Then you had to ring up your aunt and uncle. I had to sit on the side of the road. I was like, 'I can't go home because I just had all this trauma leaving.' We spent the afternoon—
>
> Tim: We had to go to the car wreckers and get all the parts.
>
> Jane: Cars are much safer now. You don't see that happening anymore. There's a lot to be said for Japanese imports.

The day she left home, Jane's mother had tearfully given her a hundred dollars — a safety net so she would have the bus fare to come back home if she wanted to. Jane and Tim spent it on rent, and settled into life together. By April 1978 — less than a year after they met — they were married with their first child on the way, and Tim was properly welcomed into the family. 'Jane's parents hated me, particularly her mother, for the first year or so, and then it completely flipped the other way, and we were fully supported and everyone said, "What a good match."' By the time Jane turned 21, they had three kids. 'Which was pretty cool,' says Tim. 'Scary,' says Jane. Four decades later, there are grandchildren, too.

Sitting now at their kitchen table, there's this really glorious moment when I ask Tim and Jane whether they remember the specific date of the first time they met — the whack on the ankle and the trip to A&E. Tim gets a weird look on his face, and I think he might be embarrassed about being put on the spot — like there was suddenly a test he hadn't studied for. But Jane leaps up from the kitchen table and tears off into the living room shouting, 'This is how romantic he is!' over her shoulder. She comes back with a handcrafted wooden box, the size and shape of a small footstool. 'He made this in woodworking class in high school, and he put that on it.' Jane opens the hinged lid of the treasure box and on the inside, with a hot poker, 18-year-old Tim has written *Jane, I love you xxx* with a heart etched beside it. And at the bottom there's the date they first met: *11.6.77.* This was the thing Tim was proudest about making at school and, as soon as they met, he had made it hers. It is the sweetest thing you could ever hope to see. They celebrate their April wedding anniversary with dinners or trips away. But there's always a moment every June 11 when they take a moment to say to each other, 'We've known each other for this many years.' A smaller, quiet, more intimate celebration, just for them.

When I drive home later that night (no breakdowns), there's an email waiting for me from Tim. There were two things they had forgotten to tell me while we were sitting at the kitchen table. One was about a moment at their wedding in 1978 when, immediately after the ceremony, one of Jane's great-aunts had come over to her, sobbing, and hugged Jane and warned her that this marriage wouldn't last. Jane was understandably horrified. Tim says they've both often reflected on that moment — it's a strand that has been woven into their shared story — and they think it might have spurred them on to prove something to everyone and make their marriage work. Not that I'd advise whispering any such nonsense into the ear of a freshly minted bride — Heaven forfend! — but I do enjoy the idea that it bound them even closer.

And one other story they like to tell. After they'd been married a few years, they were sitting with some of Jane's wider family, swapping stories about how each of the couples got together and what had attracted them to each other. Jane told them, 'Tim fell in love with me for my mind.' To which her father replied, 'Well, he was looking for it in a funny place!'

Ah, those chemicals. We're going to talk chemistry a bit later, but first, we've got some weddings to go to.

CHAPTER 9

'I Go to All His Weddings'

IN ALL OF THESE CONVERSATIONS with different couples over kitchen, dining and coffee tables, the same phrases keep turning up.

There is: 'Here's a story we like to tell ...' and 'The way I like to tell it is ...' Tales told over and over again — pulled out at dinner parties, on lunch breaks, at family gatherings or when meeting new people — that have been smoothed and refined to delight their listeners, and also to say something meaningful about who the storytellers are.

There is also: 'I don't know if I've ever told you this, but ...' from one person to their long-time partner. It fascinates me that, in the process of consciously digging down into your memories while under a bit of audience pressure (there's an interviewer in the room with a recorder), a new, separate memory can be unearthed and shared with your partner for the first time. No matter how settled your narrative is, you can find fresh details to add.

Often there is: 'I don't remember that!' / 'I do!' — Martin's pickled cucumbers and Soraya's bottle of bourbon — which tells us that two people at the same event can have quite different memories of it, or none at all. You can only assume that either one of them has imagined something, or the other has banished it from their memory, choosing to forget a thing that might not suit their version of who they are.

Most stories come with astonishingly specific visual memories, given the lapse of time — what someone was wearing 30 or 40 years ago when you first clapped eyes on them, like Belynda's dungarees and Soraya's leather jandals. And I'll be honest, I still can't get over Chris Larking's total recall of the picnic menu on the side of Aoraki/Mt Cook. 'Herbed potato salad with bacon bits'! (Which herbs, Chris? We want *details*.)

I'm still struck by the sight of three different men clearly continuing to grapple with what the hell was going on when they were hit by a sudden unbidden urge to marry (they were thrilled, yes, but remain bewildered about where that came from), and other people talking about being blindsided by some irresistible moment of 'knowing' that they had found their One In Particular.

Sometimes both people in the couple remember a pivotal moment — and appreciate that it was pivotal — yet they remember it in a remarkably different way.

All of these things happen in this next story. There is something he's never told her before; a dramatic scene she remembers, but he can't; a whole other boyfriend she has forgotten about until now; and one curiously conflicting memory.

*

Briony Ellis and **Roger Wood** were (spoiler alert) married in 1999. I'm telling you that upfront, because otherwise the story of how they got there (it took 14 effing years) is so oh-my-God-could-they-just-get-it-together-what-is-*wrong*-with-them you might have to breathe into a paper bag, or shout at the cat and go for a long walk. A full 29 minutes into listening to them describe how she was single but he wasn't; he was single, she wasn't; both were single but in the wrong cities, and then the right cities but suddenly she's not single anymore, I shouted, 'Oh, for God's sake, come *on*, you two!' quite loudly, which would have been fine except we were sitting in the very public front bar of Wellington's Museum Hotel at the time. Apologies to all the Happy Hour guests.

We are talking the dramatic arc and sexual tension of *Friends*' Ross and Rachel — although visually you might want to picture Chandler and Monica. Roger (Briony calls him

'Rog', as in 'Rodge') is one of those men who doesn't think of himself as a Hot Dude (he says as much at one point), which is attractive in itself, but he is totally enchanting once he relaxes, and particularly so when he's talking about something he really cares about. Like Briony. He is totally into Briony. Remember that thing I said in Chapter 4 about how there is nothing a woman finds more attractive than a man who is in love with his wife? That.

Briony is chestnut-haired with startlingly blue eyes. I've known her since the early 1980s, and I'm still startled by the blueness of those eyes whenever I see her. That and her laugh — Briony was always, in our student days, the most ladylike, cultured and well behaved of us, and then she would explode with the kind of laugh that seems totally involuntary, as though she just can't help herself. Roger says it's a laugh that makes you feel like you're the funniest person in the world. She and I haven't seen each other for years — this is the first time I've met Roger — so their story is all new to me. These days, Briony is a consultant for festivals and events, and Roger is a manager at Sport NZ. Which is not far from where they were when they met — just the more grown-up version.

In 1984, Briony was employed as the Director of the New Zealand Students' Arts Council (NZSAC), the national body which toured hot fresh talent like the Topp Twins and Limbs

Dance Company to university and other tertiary campuses around the country. Recently graduated, I was working for the New Zealand Society of Master Plumbers and Gasfitters as their in-house journalist in the same building as NZSAC on Wellington's Courtenay Place. (Yeah, one of us was living the dream.) Briony and I were in neighbouring offices, and one of her co-workers was my flatmate. You could occasionally hear Briony's laugh explode on the other side of the wall.

Meanwhile, in Christchurch, Roger was Sports Officer for the University of Canterbury Students' Association, and briefly also their acting Cultural Affairs Officer — so an elected student politician, but more interested, he says, in sport and cultural life than in your actual student politics.

It was the fashion then that, every few years, one or other of the individual universities would threaten to pull out of national bodies like the Students' Arts Council (or Sports Union or national Students' Association) to save on fees and have a crack at doing it on their own. Roger calls it, as generously as he can manage, 'rationalisation of spend'. In 1985, it was Canterbury's turn to threaten to withdraw from NZSAC. The board sent Briony down to try to change their minds.

'They sent this glorious, gorgeous thing,' he says, looking at Briony, 'to twist everyone's arm.' She says she was terrified at the thought of standing up in the quad in front of the assembled students to explain the value of the Students' Arts Council and how it cost them no more than a cup of coffee per student to join for the whole year. (This is back when measuring things in cups of coffee was novel and inspiring. Also, coffee was cheaper.)

Roger had the job of meeting and greeting her when she arrived on campus — possibly because (and this is a total surprise to her now) he was actually on her side. The executive was split, and he'd voted against withdrawing. 'You never told me that!' she says, possibly adoring him even a little more.

Together, they describe the exact moment they first saw each other. Except ...

Briony: I knew where I had to go to meet with the person who had been assigned to look after me once I got onto campus, and bowling down the stairs came Rog.

Roger: I remember it the other way. I remember being at the bottom of the stairs and you being at the top.

Briony: Oh, really? That's interesting. I remember being at the bottom of the stairs and you standing at the top of the stairs.

Roger: Well, that *is* interesting. Because I remember being at the bottom of the stairs looking up.

Yeah, this goes on for a while. The memory is vivid for each of them, but they can't both be right. Here's the only way I can explain it: there is something symbolic about looking up at someone at the top of a flight of steps with the light behind them as they come down towards you, like they are descending from the heavens to land in your world. Flip the perspective around and it's not quite the same. They have both managed to *see* it as the other person arriving from somewhere above them because that's how it *felt*.

At first, Roger didn't even know that this was *the* Briony Ellis who worked for NZSAC, and she didn't know who he was, but there was an instant connection, reaching, Roger says, the length of the staircase from one single look.

> Briony: What I remember was his *eyes*.
>
> Roger: I remember *her* eyes.
>
> Briony: Oh … That's quite gorgeous.
>
> Roger: It *was* quite gorgeous. Yes.

Which was all fine and dandy, but both of them were already in relationships, so, despite each feeling 'zapped', nothing happened that day except the meeting of the general student body. Briony put her case (with a fair deal of help from Roger's leading and supportive line of questioning) and won the battle, but not the war. Ultimately, Canterbury withdrew. It forced the beginning of a restructure of NZSAC into something more streamlined, and a year or so later Briony resigned to do other things. But before she left, she was given the task of showing her replacement the ropes.

The incoming director was — drumroll please — Roger Wood. This required Roger to move up to Wellington and work alongside Briony for three months. They still have their business cards from that changeover period on a pin-board at home — identical apart from their names. They were acutely aware something important was going on between them — a 'connection', they both say several times — but avoided making any kind of relationship decisions until it reached the time when Roger's girlfriend was due to move up from Christchurch to join him. Briony remembers the day they decided not to be with each other. Roger doesn't.

'It's completely blank,' he says. 'I have no memory of this at all. It surprises me every time she tells me that this happened.' He doesn't sound at all disbelieving as he says this, just very sorry and sad.

Briony's story then. 'Rog used to ride a motorbike. There is only one person I would ever sit on the back of a motorbike with, and that's Rog. He has always ridden motorbikes, and I sometimes ride with him, but I've never been on anyone else's motorbike and I never will. Anyway, he had a motorbike and we went on a ride out to Makara beach.' Which is where Roger told her he had to continue his relationship with his girlfriend, and he and Briony would have to stop spending time with each other. 'He is a very loyal man,' she says. 'I was devastated.'

I ask Roger whether he remembers even making the trip to Makara. He shakes his head. 'It's remarkable, isn't it? The interesting thing is that, even though you've reminded me about it so often,' he says with a smile, 'I still think of it as, if anything, a dream. I can't picture myself in that position, doing that, at all.' Briony says the other possibility is that he didn't actually say it quite the way she remembers, 'But I definitely felt cast adrift at that point.' And Roger says, 'I can't imagine you ever being cast adrift by anyone.' They're looking at each other so hard, I get the sense they've both entirely forgotten that there is anyone else in the front bar right now.

Roger settles into life in Wellington, doing the job Briony used to do. He had his girlfriend; Briony had other relationships; and all of them now belonged to the same broad group of friends. Briony says she consciously turned her feelings towards him into a protective, brother/sister thing. And in the process of convincing herself that she no longer had romantic feelings for Roger, she managed to convince him, too. 'Part of that was I couldn't believe that she would,' he says with genuine humility.

'That was the key to it. I've always said that. Remarkable to believe. I still can't believe it.'

In 1989, when Roger got married, naturally his buddy Briony was invited to the wedding. She had the most horrendous dream the night before. 'It was a nightmare, actually a nightmare.' The details are lost now. I ask if she was tempted to stand up and shout 'It should have been me!' during the ceremony, and on reflection she thinks that might have been the point of the dream. Briony was, in fact, very well behaved on the day.

Roger's marriage wasn't an easy one, with many in their shared circle of friends expressing concern. Meanwhile, Briony was single and, among other things, managing Wellington soul band The Holidaymakers. On more than one occasion, Roger says, he would engineer contact with her by turning up at their gigs — which is news to her. 'Did you?' she says, surprised and a bit pleased. She does remember warm chats they'd have with each other about their respective relationship ups and downs. They remained firmly in the Friend Zone.

Then Roger and his wife travel overseas for a mix of work and OE. She comes back first — pregnant and unwell — with Roger not far behind. Their daughter, Jess, is born in 1992. They separate in 1994.

Roger is single in Wellington. Briony is neither of those things. She has moved south to establish the Christchurch

Arts Festival, and is in an on-again-off-again relationship with someone who she says is jealous of virtually every man she meets (and you meet a lot of people when you're running a festival). Briony and her boyfriend at the time rent a house inland from Nelson for Christmas, and Roger and his small daughter come to stay with them, pitching a tent in the garden. Unusually, they both say, Briony's partner doesn't see Roger as any kind of threat. 'It's because I'm so boring. And unattractive,' Roger says, and Briony does one of her explosive laughs. They were fooling everyone with this brother/sister thing, including themselves.

Roger and his wife reconcile and buy a house, then separate for the final time in 1996. Single once more, he visits his pal Briony in Christchurch. This time there is an undeniable spark, but ... Briony is on again with the on-again-off-again boyfriend. It was at about this point that I shouted, 'Oh, for the love of God!' No doubt you're feeling it, too, yes? Well, strap in.

By late 1997, they are both single (Yay!) but living in different cities (Boo!), when Briony lands a contract to do the opening of Te Papa in Wellington. 'The opening day was 14 February 1998, so I was commuting up here from October onwards while still doing the Christchurch Arts Festival at home. I was finally spending time in Wellington, Rog was in Wellington; I was available, he was available ...'

Roger: And just when it became almost a reality, she went off and got another boyfriend.

Briony: Oh, that's right, I did, too! That's true! I forgot about that!

Roger: We were ready to launch into a full-flung relationship where everything was perfect ... And she hooked up with someone else!

Briony: I'd forgotten all about that!

Me: God, you're hopeless.

Briony: I know.

Roger: I thought, 'Oh well, it wasn't meant to be.'

Briony: I had forgotten all about that.

Roger: I hadn't! [*hearty laughter all round*]

This is a fairly dramatic turn of events that she has blanked from her memory, although not entirely a 'Makara moment', because she does remember it now that Roger brings it up. 'Honestly, it probably lasted a month!' But it was perfectly the wrong time, Roger says. He took it as a sign that she really wasn't that into him. She explains it as a test, not of Roger, but of herself. She'd spent the best part of 13 years fighting her romantic feelings for Roger, and now allowing herself to feel them felt wrong, so she put up a barrier between them in the shape of a new boyfriend. To be fair, it had taken some effort in 1986 to transition her feelings into a brother/sister relationship, so transitioning out of it was going to take some effort, too. Luckily for them (and for us, Dear Reader) Roger waited patiently and — ta-da! — by Christmas 1997, they were A Couple.

It was a magical Christmas. Briony's PA — who, like many of their mutual friends, was a cheerleader for the Wood/Ellis union — booked a fishing lodge in Waterfall Bay in the Marlborough Sounds, and their whole gang turned up for New Year to watch shooting stars and feast on freshly caught cod. By the time Te Papa opened in February, Roger was right beside Briony, making sure she was fed and watered and generally supported, and they spent the rest of 1998 commuting to each other's cities.

A marathon romance like this deserves a spectacular marriage proposal, and it got one. It takes place during the jazz and cabaret season at Briony's last Christchurch Arts Festival, in 1999. Roger has come down for it, and Briony's father is also there, visiting from his home in Denmark. Roger has met Stead once before — he'd been on a business trip to Copenhagen a few months earlier, and had, without Briony knowing it, planned to ask Stead then for his daughter's hand in marriage. It was an old-school tradition that Roger guessed Stead would appreciate. But somehow, in Copenhagen it hadn't felt right — Roger was aware that Stead had never seen the two of them together, and it's hard to bless a union you haven't witnessed. So Roger flew home without the question being asked.

And now, here Stead was in New Zealand. Roger took him out for a beer and found the right words to ask, and Stead found the right answer. He also confided to Roger that he'd had the answer ready during those awkward moments in Copenhagen. Dads aren't stupid.

The next evening, Briony is up to her eyeballs in the usual festival frenzy, taking care of front-of-house business. She loves this festival, and she's proud of it, and Roger has been doing that thing again of making sure she is fed and watered, and letting her know how proud he is of her success. On her own for a moment in the midst of getting on with it, surrounded by audience buzz and live jazz, Briony finds a card Roger has tucked underneath the ticketing box. In her own time, she reads it. It's his proposal. She has whole minutes to absorb this and celebrate it in her own heart before finding Roger. He asks her the question — out loud this time — and they're engaged.

Once the festival is put away, they load up her car and his car, and drive in convoy to Wellington, where they have remained ever since. Their wedding in 1999 featured many of the same players as Roger's first wedding in 1989. In a speech, one of their friends said, 'I go to all of Roger's weddings,' at which point Briony was able to heckle, 'So do I!' Roger's daughter, Jessie, is a big part of their lives, and they have a daughter together, Milla, born in 2001. For years, they say, they didn't tell people about that first meeting on the stairs — out of respect for Roger's then-girlfriend — but they have woven it back into their story because, for them, it is a remarkable and treasured moment. Just weeks before we meet at the Museum Hotel, the quake-damaged student union building in Christchurch had been demolished, and it had affected both of them deeply. They'd even considered travelling down to bear witness to it. 'We were so sad about it,' Roger says. 'That was a huge part of my life.' 'A huge part of your life, and a hugely significant place for us,' Briony says.

I ask whether they have any regrets about the winding roads and — let's be honest — cul-de-sacs on their romantic journey. Roger says something that echoes what Patrick says in Chapter 7. 'The interesting thing is that it was all about "the right time". All of those things were not the right time. It didn't mean that the intensity and the feelings were bad, it was just there were other things happening, and in fact you had to go away again for a while, while time moved on and things happened and you had more experiences. But it never really changed the underlying, core feelings. Nothing did. Right through the whole thing.'

And still nothing does, Briony says. 'Marriages have their moments when you think "that was a big argument", but nothing ever changes the underlying thing. It's rock solid.' You reach a point, I say, where walking away is off the table and you get on with working it out, right? Briony also thinks it makes a difference that they've known each other pretty much all of their adult lives, so how could they regret those years of platonic friendship? 'It's not necessarily something that we talk about in those terms, but it's something that is certainly the basis of our relationship — that we know each other as well as we know ourselves. We've been best friends for a long time.'

Which makes, they say, celebrating their wedding anniversary somewhat anti-climactic — years married doesn't accurately represent years in each other's orbit. I suggest they work out the date of that student meeting and stick it on their calendar. They consider this for a moment and break into grins. 'It's quite good looking back on the sexy bits, isn't it?' Roger says. And there's that laugh exploding out of Briony again.

*

Even before I met with Briony and Roger, I was getting a pretty clear message that 'memory' is not just about hard facts and clinical record-keeping. My instincts told me there's a creative aspect to remembering important events — the details you leave out and the elements you choose to bring in. I wanted to know more about how we create memories — what is happening in our brain when we record an event and then when we retrieve it later on. So I made an appointment with a brain expert to talk about the science behind the storytelling.

CHAPTER 10

The Brainy Stuff

YOU KNOW YOU'RE GETTING OLD when a university professor agrees to meet with you because she used to watch you on TV when she was a kid. To be fair, I think Donna Rose Addis is so curious about anything to do with memory she was genuinely intrigued by the questions I sent her, but still, it was nice to think she'd been watching *ThunderCats* while I bounced around the *What Now?* studio with my whacky topknot back in the day.

Professor Addis is a neuroscientist who leads The Memory Lab at the University of Auckland. In the years since she watched *What Now?*, she has earned a PhD at the University of Toronto and a fellowship at Harvard, and won several awards, including the prestigious Prime Minister's MacDiarmid Emerging Scientist Prize in 2010. She would get the role of 'neuroscientist' in a TV drama only if the producers decided to cast outside the stereotype — she's young, attractive, warm, funny; not at all pointy-headed or metaphorically dipped-in-formaldehyde. I reckon she'd be a hoot at Friday drinks.

It's a relief that she's so welcoming and relaxed, because my walk through Auckland's campus to her office takes me back to my pre-*What Now?* student-self, who might have been nervous about a meeting with a professor. This wasn't my campus (I went to Victoria), but the architecture in this block is identical to Vic's student union building, and there's something about the glass and steel, the old linoleum, lifts out-of-order, and long corridors with nameplates on doors that makes me feel 18 and possibly in deep trouble for missing an essay deadline. That didn't happen often, but, decades later, I have recurring anxious dreams about not handing in papers, and even worse nightmares about sitting exams for courses I haven't attended. The dreams are so vivid that, 30 years after graduation, I have to talk my cold-sweaty-self through it in the morning.

Donna Rose's office looks like any academic's workspace, except that, scattered among the books and files, there are several plastic-model brains with sections that come apart. They look as though they'd be fun to play with, like giant Happy Meal toys. Trying not to touch anything, I ask Donna Rose to explain how our brains work in terms of encoding and retrieving memories of important events. Everything that followed was news to me (there was bugger-all neuroscience in my English Literature and Drama degree), and so, because of the way my brain works in processing new information (which is to use similes and metaphors), I'm going to explain it to you like this …

Imagine that your brain is a room. Specifically, imagine that it is an office and that it is filled with information which you store in file boxes. There are labels on those boxes. They say things like 'visual detail', 'smells', 'sounds', 'emotional detail', 'spatial layout', 'who was there', 'what people said', and so on. Now, when an event occurs, we record all of those different elements and file them carefully in the appropriate boxes in our brain-office. So a memory of, for example, last Christmas isn't stored in one place in your brain — it is stored in several places: the smells of the tree and the baked ham are in one box; what the gifts and decorations looked like are in another; what your aunt said after three wines is in another box; and how you felt about that is somewhere else.

When you ask your brain to recall 'last Christmas', here's what happens: your hippocampus behaves like a loyal and faithful Personal Assistant. It runs around the office, grabbing all the relevant bits from each of those individual file boxes — what you saw, what you heard, what you tasted — then collates them neatly into one file and places it on your desk. To the naked eye, it appears that the memory comes back to us all joined-up and seamless, but actually the hippocampus has been very busy — grabbing visual details from the box in the posterior parts of the brain-office, and the emotional details and smells from the boxes in your sensory cortex, and so on. You don't have to ask your hippocampus to do this — it's just what a good PA does.

Pulling all those bits out of different places in your brain is called 'episodic memory', and while it is happening it feels a lot like you are re-experiencing the event, as though it is 'unfolding' in your brain again. Sometimes it is so much like reliving the experience that you will even slip into using the present tense as you talk about it. 'I walked into the room … And then I'm staring at the most beautiful tree I've ever seen!' That kind of thing.

Episodic memory is a flexible and dynamic process, which means you won't necessarily remember last Christmas the same way every time you call it up. Your hippocampus might go looking in the boxes in a different order, or might forget to look in a box, or even pull the wrong thing out. It could, perhaps, go for 'last Christmas' in the 'smells' box and accidentally take out 'turkey' which in fact belonged to the Christmas before. It's good, your hippocampus, but it's only human.

What gets remembered can also be affected by your current mood — something called 'mood congruence' in tech-speak.

If you are in your happy place, your hippocampus might be more likely to dig out the positive memories of the event — the highly successful trifle, or the nice thing your partner said. But if you're already in a negative mood, you might be more likely to recall the anti-cellulite cream someone stuck a bow on and left for you under the tree.

The running-around-the-room thing to put 'last Christmas' together in an episodic way will happen over and over again, sometimes with these slight variations in the results. But eventually, after you've remembered an event and told the story many times, it will stop being recalled as a flexible 'episodic' memory and become a fixed 'semantic' memory instead.

'Semantic memories are more fact-like,' Donna Rose explains. 'You can imagine if you have somebody who recalls a memory and they recall it in the exact same way every single time, you can pretty much guarantee that those are semanticised memories now. My grandma will have certain stories that she'll always tell, and they always play out the exact same way. They've become almost folklore, like a little folk story for her.'

These semantic memories are filed away in your anterior temporal lobe — basically that's the pub-quiz part of your brain. This is where you'll find the answers to questions like 'What is the capital of Romania?' and 'How many points is the green ball worth in snooker?', but you can also find facts about your own life there, like your eftpos PIN, the names of your kids, and some favourite stories.

As you get older, you get better at semanticised memory and less good at episodic memory. That can be because your PA gets a tad bored with poking around in those boxes for the same old stuff, and also because as she gets closer to retirement age she's not so nimble around the brain-office, so you might be inclined to let her take longer breaks while you just reach for the facts. But, Donna Rose says, you might also begin to rely more on semantic memory because you've lived so long that the goal of communication has changed — you reach a point in your life (or with a particular story) where you're into its broad themes rather than the little details. 'You might choose to tell only certain parts of a memory to give it meaning in the context of your life,' Donna Rose explains. In her world, this is called 'meaning-making'.

As she says this, I let out a little 'whoop' of delight and present her with my theory from right back at the beginning of this book: that we use stories to make sense of the chaos of our lives. The childbirth story, for example, where we take the good and hopeful and maybe the dramatic elements to say something good, hopeful and dramatic about the arrival of this new human on the planet. We keep the bits that support the story we want to tell, and allow the bits that are extraneous to a good and hopeful story to fall away. Professor Addis agrees: she thinks this is absolutely what remembered stories are for, to make sense of — and give meaning to — what might otherwise be chaos.

Let's just pause here for a moment while I roll around in the joy of an eminent and award-winning neuroscientist giving her thumbs-up to my fundamental theory of life and the role of storytelling in it.

Isn't that nice? Right, carry on — back to Donna Rose.

For a while, she says, it might be that we actually have both types of memories coexisting — the episodic ones that unfold each time in your brain, as well as the semantic memories that you present as an often-told folktale. Then, over time, we might lose the more detailed ones and just stay with the semanticised ones. But this doesn't mean that you can't remember the little details if you want to — they are still stored in the boxes in your brain-office. You might have a family story you love to tell, but, if you're challenged to, you may be able to access your episodic memory and find some new bits. I tell her this would explain those 'I don't know if I've ever told you this ...' moments where one half of a couple suddenly unearths some new memory. Think of Patrick and Maria and their suddenly remembered epiphany in the supermarket snack aisle. While fossicking around in the boxes where they'd filed that trip out to Anawhata and the near-drowning, they'd stumbled across memories they hadn't talked about to each other before. Donna Rose and I are both delighted that in the interview process they've genuinely retrieved an episodic memory rather than solely an edited and often-repeated semantic one.

It made me think, too, of the first story I told about meeting Ian and Clare in Rarotonga. I'm used to saying that we met them at a dinner at The Waterline. That's the semantic version of the story. But when I went back into my brain-office to search for detailed memories of that night, I recalled that when we'd walked into the restaurant the very first time Clare had waved at us. Why? And then I'd remembered that she waved at us because we'd met her at a café where she worked earlier that day. I had re-experienced the memory in an episodic way and found a tiny detail I'd let go of, because it hadn't mattered — the dinner was the significant meeting. So I'd left out lunch from the semanticised story, yet the episodic memory was still there if I looked for it. (Donna Rose fairly clapped her hands with joy when I reported this to her. I was so impressed, I gave my hippocampus the rest of the day off.)

When I ask Donna Rose about the great mystery of how two people at the same event can remember it in different ways, she explains something that is suddenly obvious. First, we *experience* it in different ways right at the start: physically we are standing in different spots, so the view is literally different.

Second, we will lay down the memory differently — what our own PA decides to place in the file boxes will be specific to us, too. In a highly emotional situation, the hippocampus will be either frantically trying to record every detail, or it might get so overloaded that it can't manage to file some things at all, or it might deliberately choose not to stick some details in boxes. I'm thinking that's what happened to Roger that day in Makara — his hippocampus decided that telling Briony they couldn't be together was too traumatic a memory for him to keep.

Even if they're not in a highly emotional state, the couple's two brain-offices will end up storing some of the exact same things, some different things, and one of them might also file something the other missed. Like two students at a lecture taking different notes.

Third, add to that the retrieval process — you've got two PAs running around completely separate offices, delving into boxes that hold diverse things — and you can appreciate there is plenty of opportunity for the two final memory-documents to look dissimilar to some degree. Plus, you will (consciously or unconsciously) edit out details you don't like, or that don't fit the story you want to tell in terms of meaning-making and finding order in the chaos. Then, by the time you've remembered the event a few times, whatever you've left out of your story can feel like it never happened.

At this point you might be feeling overwhelmed with how 'flexible' and 'dynamic' or just downright 'unreliable' memory might be. It doesn't seem like the most efficient tool for record-keeping, right? And that's because, Professor Addis says, memory is not about record-keeping — it's about reconstructing your past. It really is (and I don't want to harp on with how right I was about this) about 'meaning-making'.

'There's certainly research that shows that we edit memories to reflect our current sense of self,' Donna Rose says. 'If things that we experienced aren't congruent with who we think we are, then we might leave parts of those memories out or we might edit those memories to reflect that.' I honestly don't know if Soraya really told Jim that The Girlfriend couldn't have any of her bourbon but, if she did, the fact she can't remember it could be explained this way: Soraya is, in all other aspects of her life, a kind and generous person, so denying anyone a hoon on her bottle of bourbon is out of character, and a memory she might choose to (a) not file away or (b) not retrieve. Also (c), Jim might just be having her on.

There's a lovely moment when I tell Donna Rose about Roger and Briony both vividly remembering the other standing at the top of the stairs when they first met. 'That's so fascinating. I wonder ... Something that can happen is that you can distort your memories by *imagining* something that didn't actually happen in that way. We do that all the time. And if imaginations are vivid, it can be very difficult to tell apart what's real and what's not. We've all had that experience where we've had a dream and it's so vivid that it keeps coming back to you, and you're like, "Did that actually happen or did it not?"'

Like that dream about sitting an exam you haven't studied for and waking up in a cold sweat, right?

When that happens, Donna Rose says, our brain tries to help out by using a shortcut: it tells us that if we can picture something really vividly, then it must have happened. So in Roger and Briony's case, Donna Rose suggests that whoever was at the bottom of the stairs must have talked about it so powerfully, the other has visualised their version, and then adopted it as their own.

'Over time the other person has *imagined* that moment from the other person's perspective, they've imagined what it was like to be at the bottom of the stairs looking up, and then they've actually *overwritten* their own memory of how they met,' she says. I tell her I think that's really cute — that you can adore someone so much that their memory of an event is more powerful than your own. 'It's *so* cute,' she says, 'I love that. That's so cool.'

So maybe, rather than being surprised about minor differences in detail, we should be impressed with how much all of these couples' stories actually match. What that means, Donna Rose says, is that they've been communicating openly with each other in the early phase of rehearsing their memories, crafting them collaboratively to make a story that represents them both. I describe to Donna Rose how dozens of my interviews have begun with me looking at them both and asking, 'So … how did you two meet?' Immediately, one of them will start talking while the other sits calmly and listens — they both know how the story goes, and who will start it. Eventually, the one who started talking first will look at their partner and say, 'And now you tell her the next bit.' It's as if, I tell Donna Rose, they hold different parts of the story, and cue the other for the next chapter.

'That's so fascinating,' Donna Rose says. 'There's a really interesting thing where couples end up having a memory that is greater than the sum of the parts, right? Each individual might actually hold parts of the story, and so it's only when they're together that you get the full story. This what we call "extended cognition" or "extended memory". It exists beyond your own mind, so that you actually need that other person there to get the full story.'

In a sense, then, the other person in a couple-story is playing the role of your hippocampus — helping to direct the search into the boxes in our brain to retrieve pieces of the story you might otherwise miss. I tell Donna Rose about an interview that didn't go so well — a widow who wanted to share her story, but kept getting lost with what happened next. Maybe she ran out of steam because she'd reached the part of the story her late-husband used to tell? This makes sense to Donna Rose: she was involved in a study in Sydney with older adults, which showed that their ability to recall memory was so much richer when they talked together as a couple rather than separately — filling in each other's gaps, and helping each other unearth a forgotten thing. A colleague in Sydney is using this couple-based 'extended cognition' to help patients with dementia.

I think about this power-of-two months later when I write back to people like Gavin 'stoat-trapper' Schist and John 'the wrong room' Bannock, who emailed their 'How We Met' story independently of their partners. Once I had encouraged them to show the story to their wives before it was committed to print, they both came back with more details — not different versions, just richer descriptions of what went down. They'd been cued by their partners to recall a deeper memory.

Not all storytelling, Donna Rose says, is good for us. There is 'savouring', but there is also 'rumination'. 'Rumination' is dwelling on the shitty stuff, and the over-generalities. Those nasty phrases in your interior monologue like 'Nobody ever likes me, I'm always left out', with a story attached to that thesis that proves it is true — at least in one instance.

'Savouring', on the other hand, is what we do with much more detailed memories about significant events. 'How you met your partner is one of those. They capture, maybe crystallise, that sense of who you are, or who you are with your partner — in terms of bonding, or reigniting, or maintaining.'

I tell Donna Rose my other big theory — that having a shared story binds us together — and again, I have the glorious experience of a layperson's observation being validated by neuroscience. Honestly, it's like getting an A+ for an essay. 'I think telling stories about specific experiences that you've had together is probably very bonding. It's like having a shared folklore, and no doubt that sets the tone or the identity of the relationship. I think that would actually carry them forward into the future together as well. That's probably one of the reasons why we have such good episodic memories, and the reason why we like to talk about our memories with other people. It's such a reinforcing thing to sit around and reminisce. That helps you bond with people and find those commonalities.'

Savouring, then. Sitting around and reminiscing about how two people fell in love. This seems like a good time to go visit Maeve and Declan, who are having a tough time, and talk about how a girl from Donegal met a boy from Waipū at a barbecue in Perth, and their secret, scandalous start.

CHAPTER 11

'Don't Be Too Polite'

I WAS RAISED ON GOOD MANNERS — the right thing to say, which knife to use at dinner, the appropriate behaviour and acceptable language for polite company. What I like about rules, and laws, and codes of social conduct is that, if you understand them properly, you also know when it is a fucking great idea to ignore the shit out of them.

A couple of years ago, my mother reminded me of a story I had completely forgotten. It had happened during a visit home from university in 1980. Raised not just on good manners but also with a sense of social justice passed down through many generations, I'd taken up at Victoria with a fabulous band of feminists, socialists and communists who also wanted to Change The World And Make It A Better Place. A fair bit of my life was spent going along to rallies against student fees (I'm sorry that didn't work out) and protests against the 1981 Springbok Tour, or to support workers' strikes or call for homosexual law reform. For a while there, I was involved in agitprop theatre, and I can still bellow out a lusty rendition of 'Bread and Roses' and snippets of the much-lesser-known anti-capitalist song 'The World's Your Oyster'. One song which challenged my young, female, petit bourgeois, people-pleasing self was Australian folksinger and songwriter Glen Tomasetti's union ditty 'Don't Be Too Polite, Girls'. In her lyrics, Tomasetti urges women to stop being so bloody nice about pay inequality, to not 'be fearful of offending in case you get the sack / just recognise your value and ... you-won't-look-back!' Ba-da-da-bum. It's heaps catchy.

Emboldened by all this student activism, I must have been trying out a few of my political theories on my mother and expressing them with some of the new language I'd picked up on the frontlines. Whatever it was, we were in the kitchen and I said 'fuck' in front of my mother. Using my full name (a rarity — I was clearly in trouble) she said, 'Michèle! I will not have that kind of language in my drawing room!' To which I replied with all the confidence of an 18-year-old socialist-feminist who has been on one or two marches and is studying political science and therefore knows everything, 'That's all right, Mum — we're in the fucking kitchen.'

Even as a grown-up, I still relish the idea that a touch of well-placed explosive language or occasional inappropriate behaviour can be inordinately effective in cutting through. It is also wise to be wary of constantly sticking to the rules if you want life to be less ordinary. My eye continues to be drawn to other versions of Tomasetti's admonishment to not be 'too polite'. Just recently, after an emotional day at the National Civil Rights Museum in Memphis (built around the motel where Martin Luther King Jr was murdered), I bought fridge magnets and badges for my girlfriends, emblazoned with Laurel Thatcher Ulrich's statement: 'Well Behaved Women Seldom Make History'. It seems I keep needing to remind myself that to get things done and to make your world a better place, you might need to break some rules.

I ignored the shit out of my '15-years-together' rule to put **Declan** and **Maeve** in this book, and I couldn't be happier about that. They broke a few rules themselves when they got together in 2008, and they couldn't have been happier about that either. They'd kept their story a secret until we sat down with cups of tea and shortbread in November 2015.

A few days earlier, Declan had been talking to our mutual friend, Dan (Declan's best buddy and the celebrant at their wedding), about me coming over to get their story. He told Dan that he and Maeve were still not sure whether they should tell me 'the true version or the fake version'. Declan tells me: 'Dan goes, "What do you mean 'the true version'?" Because he'd had to read out the fake version at the wedding.'

They might not have told their real story to other people, but they talk about it a lot with each other. They treasure it, relive all the moments, feel all the feels they had from the first instant they met. 'Because it's a *story*, you know?' Declan says. Other relationships start because your friends know each other, or you drink in the same pub, or you just 'fall into it' with someone. But this was different. 'The story makes me laugh and cry at the same time,' Maeve says. Life has been exciting and so awesome, Declan says, from the day he first saw Maeve. And then he qualifies it. 'Other than getting cancer. Apart from that little hurdle ...' We all try laughing at this. 'Other than that little fucking thing,' Maeve adds brightly, 'it's been bloody brilliant.'

When we talk in 2015, Declan is managing a recruitment company and Maeve is an IT project manager. She's Irish, from a little town in Donegal called Muff. 'Muff!' Declan exclaims, and you can tell he's spent the past seven years enjoying the fact her hometown is a euphemism for a lady-place. '*You're* from a little town called Waipū, so I don't know what you're talking about!' Maeve counters, as she no doubt has once or twice before. Maeve is one of those raven-haired Celtic beauties — she could easily pass as the fourth sister of The Corrs. Declan's no slug either — there's a passing resemblance, I've always thought, to Jake Gyllenhaal on one of Jake's good days.

They are terrific party people. Jeremy and I have shared cabs home with Declan and Maeve from various boozy pub nights and music gigs — theirs is on the way home to ours — and there is always generous drunken haggling over who will settle the fare. 'Pay the driver, Declan!' Maeve would insist. 'No, we've got this!' Jeremy would declare, while the driver rolled his eyes, just wishing someone would get it sorted.

When Declan is diagnosed with cancer not long after their 2014 wedding, everyone is devastated. You try to think of helpful things to do, right? I'm shit at casseroles and baking, but I thought maybe an afternoon sitting in the sun and talking about how they fell in love might be a nice distraction for them both. An opportunity for savouring. Which is when they decided to tell the true story for the first time, and I got to see a grown man blush.

Back in 2008, Declan was 30 and living with his cousin in Perth. Maeve was 25 and working with the cousin's partner, which is how she was invited over to their place one afternoon for a barbecue, along with her boyfriend. Declan immediately noticed Maeve; she instantly clocked him. 'We're still arguing over whether I chased her or she chased me. I'm not really sure … I reckon she was chasing me,' he grins. And then Declan goes on to describe in minute detail exactly what Maeve was wearing that day: she'd just been for a swim at the beach so there was a blue sundress and jandals with the outline of a wet bikini underneath, which was 'pretty cute'. We all agree that the 'who was chasing whom' question might have just been answered. Then Maeve recounts how, later that evening among a crowd of people (including the boyfriend), she couldn't take her eyes off Declan. 'He was playing the guitar and kept playing these lovely songs, and I was just ...' She drifts off into a happy sigh. 'The more wines that kept going down, the more I thought, "Ah, he's so gorgeous".' 'Yeah, see?' Declan leaps in. '*She* was chasing *me*.'

For the record, Maeve recalls that Declan was wearing a red checked shirt, black skinny jeans and his Chucks — the legendary Converse high-tops he wore to every music gig with his pal, Dan. And clearly other auspicious occasions.

Not long after the cousin's barbecue, a massive crew of Irish, Aussies and Kiwis went camping beside the Margaret River. This included Declan, Maeve and the boyfriend. Maeve describes her five-and-a-half-year relationship with the boyfriend as 'one of those ones that had gone on three years too long', but no one had yet taken the initiative to call it off. At night beside the Margaret River, people started trickling off to bed (this included the boyfriend just over there in a tent), and Declan and Maeve ended up alone by the campfire. They held hands. Which led to a bit of snogging over by the woodpile. 'It was very bad!' Maeve says — meaning the propriety of it, not the kissing itself. 'Yes, it was bad,' Declan says, 'and it got even worse.' Pashing by the wood stack led to something even more passionate in the campground shower block.

There are noticeably several emotions going on for both of them as they tell me this. One is a touch of embarrassment at their own behaviour, and also surprise and a fair sprinkling of joy at the irresistibleness of the attraction. This wasn't normal behaviour for either of them, but something powerful was going on that over-rode the usual rules. This thing between them was something different — and it mattered more than 'behaving well'.

The next day was Declan's thirty-first birthday. It was also 35 degrees, he was tragically hungover, and feeling more than a little awkward around the boyfriend. Maeve doubts the boyfriend suspected anything — they were barely talking anyway by that stage, and paid one another almost no attention. In any event, the camping trip came to an abrupt end when the whole crew was tossed out for making too much noise (which Declan and Maeve can't be blamed for — they were very discreet) and everyone went home.

This is when the romance started. Declan says it was like 'a high-school courting relationship'. His flatmates twigged that something was going on between them, but disapproved because theoretically she wasn't single, so they couldn't hang out there; Maeve soon broke up officially with the boyfriend, but they were still living in the same house while they saw out the last six weeks on their lease, so they couldn't meet there either. Instead, they'd go to movies and then have pizza, or to the beach for fish'n'chips and a bottle of wine, do a bit of necking in the car, and then he'd drop her back home. 'We dated,' Maeve says, wistfully. 'We actually *dated*!' Declan grins, clearly loving the memory. 'That was cool.' Neither of them had done old-school dating before. They loved it.

But before the lease runs out, and before they can take the next step into couple-hood, Declan's company transfers him from Perth back to Auckland. Not knowing quite where they are with each other, Maeve makes new plans with her girlfriends. There will be a campervan tour of New Zealand, then she'll go home to Ireland for a wedding, then she'll move in with some mates in Sydney. During the holiday to New Zealand, she drops in on Declan in Auckland … and stays for two weeks. It's a happy time and they 'felt right with each other', Declan says, but, you know, Maeve is sticking with her plan, right? That's what sensible people do.

Until she gets back to Sydney. She and Declan are on the phone one Saturday night (they check in with each other every day), having a few wines, talking about how much they miss each other, and how Maeve isn't as comfortable in Sydney as she thought she'd be. 'Both of us were a bit pissed on the phone, talking probably close to midnight,' Declan says. At some point before the call ended, he said pretty casually, 'Why don't you just come here?' A few hours later — 3am — the phone rang again. It was Maeve. She'd gone online and booked her ticket to Auckland and could he pick her up in five hours? 'So I did. And that was it, and then we were living together.'

Declan still marvels at how quickly it happened — thrilled, but still surprised.

'I didn't realise that she was going to go and book it straight away. I thought we might talk about it the next day.' Maeve says he had been welcome to talk about it the next day all he wanted — but face to face rather than on the phone. 'You know how I like to get things done, darling!' They're both laughing. 'Yeah, yeah. Chop, chop!' he says and then adds: 'We needed to be together. It was quite apparent.'

It's this story — the 3am phone call saying 'I'm on my way' — that was told at the wedding as the marker for the beginning of their grand passion. They chose to leave out the campfire and shagging in the showers and the boyfriend (even the secret dating) because it didn't paint them in a good light. But I love the prequel so much — two people so drawn to each other they behaved in a way they would otherwise have described as 'badly'. Maeve says there was no way she could pass up the chance to be with him at Margaret River. Declan refers to it as being like a gravitational pull. Caught up in what I would assume was a full-blown episodic memory, Declan looks at her now and says, 'You were cooing like a dove over by the wood stack.' And then collects himself and blushes bright red. Which looks good on a man who has been made thin and pale by chemotherapy.

That's the thing, really. This chat in the sunshine on their deck at home, just off the living room where Declan's hospital-supplied bed is parked near bottles of pills and painkillers, has made all of us forget there is anything amiss, I think. They've been '2008 Declan and Maeve', laughing and joshing and painting vivid pictures, savouring the memories of how they met. How could any of that be anything other than glorious?

They were married on 29 November 2014 at Waipū. It was a perfect day, they say, very much like the one we are sitting in now — calm, sunny, not a cloud in sight. They dressed up an old boatshed with white floaty fabric, little lanterns and the 75 metres of bunting Declan made by hand one night when he was pissed — the same gorgeous bunting they gave to Dan later for his own wedding to Jussi. 'You guys do really good shit when you're pissed,' I observe, meaning *all* of it, and there's much laughter all round. Maeve's parents came out from Donegal for the New Zealand wedding — a secret Declan managed to keep successfully until they just appeared in front of Maeve a week before the ceremony. A remarkable feat, Maeve says, especially given that she is 'the world's nosiest person'. There was a second wedding three weeks later in Ireland.

Maeve: 'You hear people talking about on their wedding days being really nervous and all that kind of stuff; I was *so* not nervous at all. I was just like, "This is brilliant, we're going to go and get married in front of all of our friends and family, and then we're going to drink champagne and eat seafood, and have a party and it's going to be great." I think I was the only person at our wedding who didn't cry, because I was so bloody happy.'

That kind of joy is contagious. Declan's old flatmates from Perth — the ones who had been deeply disapproving when their relationship started — met up with them again at another family wedding, and the friendship was mended.

Maeve and Declan say they're not hugely romantic people — they don't go around holding hands or any of that sort of nonsense. Declan says the proposal was 'nothing special', but I'll let you be the judge of that. They'd planned Christmas in Ireland in 2014, followed by a trip to New York, and figured that, since they were going to be with Maeve's family, why didn't they get married and make New York a honeymoon? It was time, Declan says.

And then Maeve moved things along in much the same way as she had with that 3am phone call.

Maeve: Me and my friend Penny went into Michael Hill one day and started looking at rings, and I came home and was like, 'Oh, so I tried on a few rings today.' Just kind of prompting the situation a little bit.

Declan: And I said, 'Okay, let's go and have a look at them tomorrow.'

Me: Oh, you are such a good person.

Maeve: [*laughs*] He's *such* a good person.

Declan: So we got one.

Maeve: The ring had to go and get re-sized, right? So I came home from work on the Friday, and he had gone to pick up our rings, and he had a bottle of champagne and a bunch of flowers, and I went to the kitchen and there were the rings with the champagne and the flowers and he was like 'There you go!'

Not a down-on-one-knee proposal, sure, but I can spot romance when I see it. Declan struggles to remember the date of the engagement for a moment, so Maeve helps out — 28 February

2014. Later, when he's getting tired, he can't remember how old he is now, and she helps with that, too. So sometimes, this 'little cancer hurdle' makes its presence felt. But just before I leave, when Maeve goes to get their wedding album, suddenly Declan perks up and is remembering all kinds of details: the upgrade to business class on their international flight because they had Maeve's wedding dress with them as carry-on (she had forgotten that) (the upgrade, not the dress); the hilarity of being given twin beds at their hotel on the first night of their Irish honeymoon; the earlier temptation to elope, but how glad they are that they did two proper family weddings ... That there is nothing at all to regret. 'It's been so cool, all the way,' he grins.

*

Declan died on 10 February 2016, just three months after we sat on their deck in the sunshine.

The following August, Dan had a picture of Declan's legendary Chucks tattooed onto his right shoulder. Declan had worn those shoes to 90-something concerts and had ticket stubs for them all. 'He wanted to get to 100,' Dan says, 'and then frame the Chucks with the ticket stubs around the outside. He never made it to 100, so I have them there so that he is with me at every concert I ever go to. I told him before he died that

I was going to get something with his Chucks as a tattoo, and he said, "You don't want those dirty old things on your arm." Turns out I really did.'

Maeve says she can hear Declan's voice when she reads their story, that she loves remembering how happy it made them to tell it, that she cries because such an awesome guy isn't there to read it with her. And that their reliving the story of how they met that afternoon, with shortbread and cups of tea, has itself become another memory to be savoured.

CHAPTER 12

The Pheasant-plucker's Son

THAT HEADING UP THERE is my favourite one in this book. It won't make sense yet. Very much like this whole chapter, it is a lesson in the power of perseverance.

Two people 'just knowing' the instant they see each other that they are The One is always spectacular. But what about when only *one* of you knows? What happens if you see someone across a crowded room, but their eyes don't meet yours? Or they *do* see you but, meh, they're not that fussed? Wear the buggers down! Not recommending stalking, just persistence. Faith. Self-belief. Maybe some kind of health-and-safety incident that throws you together. Or you could put something in their mashed potato.

These stories are a celebration of the people who knew they'd found The One and stood their ground until The One bloody well caught on.

*

Caroline first saw **Kate** at a Lesbian Business Association event, and the second she saw her, she 'fell madly in lust with her'. She knew Kate was on her own that night, but assumed she was already in a relationship. Later, a helpful mutual friend told her that Kate was single.

'So I manufactured an excuse to ask her to have coffee with me. Then I rang her soon afterwards, asking her out to dinner. From that night on we saw a lot of each other.' But Kate didn't want a relationship, or for them to be seen as partners. Caroline, however, just kept finding things for them to do together, reasons for them to be in each other's company. It took three months, but, eventually, Kate changed her mind. That was in 2009 — Caroline can give the exact date that Kate came to see them as a couple in the same way she did.

Neither of them wants to get married — Caroline hates being the centre of attention, so a wedding would be a terrible idea, and Kate sees marriage as a dysfunctional heterosexual custom that has its roots in treating women as property, and why would anybody want *that*? What they *do* believe in is love, fidelity and good old-fashioned lust. 'Women,' Caroline says, 'should pursue the object of their lust relentlessly!' That's going on a T-shirt.

*

When I first met **Chris Clarke**, he was CEO for World Vision, and we spent a jolly afternoon together as guests on RNZ National's *The Panel*. We agreed on pretty much every issue discussed that day, so we bonded. Later, he told me about being a young man with a crush on someone who didn't even know he existed.

'It's the late 1980s and I am a third-year law student at Canterbury University — most interested in girls, but sadly they were mostly not interested in me. Enter **Karen**: a second-year political sciences student. Blonde, vivacious and loud. The idea that a university library was a place of quiet reflection was quite lost on Karen. But it was the hair I noticed first — masses of it, and cut in the style of Annie Lennox.'

Chris elaborates on this particular moment in hair history. Lennox's duo, The Eurythmics, were at their peak right then, and so was Lennox's bold 'wedge cut' for the few who dared. 'Cut close at the nape of the neck and then rising into this glorious mop on top,' he recalls. And adds: 'The hair was complemented by red tartan trousers and wild earrings.' Karen, not Annie.

Can I just cut in here and say that anytime a man makes a wry joke about women saying they 'don't have anything to wear' (by which women mean we don't have the appropriate thing to wear *in this instance*), thereby implying that men either don't care about or don't notice what we are wearing, there is a shitload of evidence in this book to suggest that what we are wearing *totally matters*, because you are going to talk about it decades later. That is all. Apologies for the interruption. Back to the lovely Chris.

'Everything Karen did seemed to be at speed, and usually surrounded by a gaggle of others. But sadly I was not even on her radar — until Fate intervened in the form of a malfunctioning library lift.

'I was standing outside the fourth-floor library lift waiting my turn. The doors opened and there she was — all hair, earrings and tartan pants, and carrying this massive pile of books, and, for once in her life, alone. She steps out of the lift — and that is when Fate intervened. Sadly (for her, not for me) the lift had stopped just short of the fourth floor. Not seeing the gap (I say it was because she saw me; I suspect she would say it was because she was *carrying books*), Karen goes to step out of the lift and trips — sending books flying — and literally falls into my delighted (if somewhat startled) arms. I'd had years imagining what I would say to any young woman who happened to swoon into my arms, but I didn't even get the chance to say "hello" — Karen was mid-cadence through a very loud, library-stopping "Shit!"

'Not the most promising start to a relationship. I did, however, get to pick up her books, buy her a coffee, and 28 years of marriage later ...'

*

I met **Bruce** in Hamilton where I was doing a show and he was the sound technician. Soundies often aren't very chatty, but Bruce was charmingly effusive. While we were packing out the theatre afterwards, he told me about meeting his wife, **Robyn**. He described what had happened 30 years ago in the present tense, as though he was watching it unfold again in his mind's eye. (And if you go back to Chris, above, you will see flashes of the present tense there, too. Episodic memories, right?)

'Sixth floor, Victoria University library, Rankin Brown Building. You walk down the aisle, see this one woman who you know is a friend of your sister's, wearing these gorgeous glasses with very black curly hair, that nobody else could possibly love as much as you.'

Was it instant for her? 'She was too smart for that. Only blokes think with their balls. Women don't. Women of that nature take a while and consider it. The thing about Robyn is she is a very intelligent woman. I think intelligence is much more important than "sexy", because there's a lifetime's entertainment there.' And just the way he says 'a lifetime's entertainment' sounds really quite sexy. Also, please note: libraries are a hotbed of romantic encounters. Keep reading the books.

*

The first time **Māwera** met **David**, he was covered in blood and feathers, and standing in a pile of dead pheasants. She decided in that instant that he was The One for her. It took him, however, a long time to come around to the idea. But that was in 2005, and now they have a child together, and run businesses, and do community advocacy work. He is an expert hunter and fisher, but he was no match for Māwera's particular brand of hunting and fishing.

David Barrett was born and raised in New Jersey, moved to Nova Scotia as a teenager, and immigrated to New Zealand with his first wife in 2001. Strictly speaking, he is an American, but visually he perfectly fits the description of 'Canadian Mountain Man' — he doesn't just look like he *lives* on a mountain, he looks *like* a mountain. With a Master's of Science in Forestry, he came to Whakatāne for a forestry job and stayed for the trout fishing and hunting. A son, Beau, was born the year after he arrived, and a daughter, Alexi, followed in 2004. Dave 'found paradise' here in the great outdoors.

Indoors, things weren't going so well. Dave says he came home one day to find the house empty of family and furniture. He says he was devastated, hadn't seen it coming at all, and found himself in the fight of his life to keep the children in

New Zealand, and to gain shared custody. In between his forestry job, and the sidelines he had with fishing and clearing farmland of wild peacocks, turkeys and pheasants, Dave taught himself about family law so he could represent himself in legal proceedings.

Māwera Karetai was born in Christchurch, but Dunedin is home. She is Ngāi Tahu, Kāti Māmoe and Waitaha ki Te Waipounamu. Māwera moved to the North Island in 1988, and had her first son (also called David) in 1989 when she was 18. When that marriage ended in 2000, she and her son moved to Whakatāne. She's warm, and round, and sharp as a tack. These days she has a degree in Business Management, a graduate diploma in Dispute Resolution, and a Master's in Environmental Management. She teaches business, loves family, and she loves to cook. Someone should put her on a wild foods version of *Master Chef*. She'd be running the show by the end of episode two.

In 2005, around the time Dave finds himself living in an empty house, Māwera and her son are renting a house near the Whakatāne beach. Māwera is doing a teaching degree, but not loving it — she would occasionally get a hard time as a South Island Māori for looking 'white', which, she says, is a weird kind of racism. There is a project she's working on that needs some feathers. She's heard about Dave and his bird hunting, and tracks him down online and arranges to go over to his place to pick up feathers, and maybe some wild meat.

'I walked down to the garage, and there stood this remarkable creature covered in blood and feathers. He had 130 pheasants lying on the ground at his feet.' Dave points out that he was thinner then than he is now, no beard, short hair. Māwera concurs, but frames it differently. 'He was really skinny. He was so skinny, it was sad.' 'Muscular and stuff, too,' Dave insists. 'I was feeling pretty good about myself.' Māwera won't be swayed. 'Yeah, it was just sad. I thought he looked far too thin.'

Nevertheless, Māwera knew she'd found Her One. 'I just said, "Oh yes, that's me."'

She went home with his feathers and some meat he'd hunted, and invited him to come over and eat it the next weekend. Presented with a huge bowl of food, Dave had said, 'Do you expect me to eat all this?' 'I said, "Yes, I do." So he did. I thought, "Wow, he's just getting better and better." I couldn't abide a man without a healthy appetite. Cooking is my thing.'

They started hanging out, just mates. Māwera, a warrior woman from way back, threw herself into helping him with his battle for shared custody of his kids — neither of them had any experience in the field, but they learned as they went. 'She's that kind of person,' Dave says. 'She's a zealot for bad causes. She jumped on board and decided to help me learn family law and write affidavits and try to advocate for me and all that stuff. She had no idea what she was doing any more than I did. That started a thing — not "a thing" like that, just a thing where we were doing this together.' That's what Dave thought, anyway.

One day they're out fishing and Māwera gets a call from her landlord saying he wants to move back into the beach house she's renting. She can't find anywhere else to go — she had her son, plus she was also taking care of two other boys at the time. Dave says she can rent a couple of rooms at his place — she's got furniture, but no house; he's got a house without any furniture. He thinks it's a no-brainer.

'I just kept saying "no",' Māwera recalls. 'Eventually he asked me why, and so I sent him an email saying, *I don't want to come live with you because I've developed these feelings for you.* He rang me and he said, "You'll get over it."'

'You're really good with the ladies,' I tell Dave, but he's not bothered.

Dave: She moves in with her son and she started — You can't stalk somebody when you live in the same house, can you?

Māwera: No.

David: But she did.

Māwera: I totally did.

Māwera and her son moved into Dave's empty house on 5 September 2005. She remembers the date, he doesn't. 'You know the exact date?' he says, surprised. 'I do,' she says calmly. 'It's the day that changed my life.' She'd filed that detail away in her brain-office, along with these others: 'He came home from work, and there was music playing and the dinner was cooking, I'd folded his washing, and he walked into a *family*. He left a house, and he walked into a *home*. You could see this look on his face that told you how he felt about that. It blew him away, and he didn't expect it to be like that, I suppose.'

With help from Māwera, Dave won shared custody of his kids, and the house filled up. Even so, Māwera still had her room, Dave had his. 'We were like that for a long time. He knew that I didn't get over it at all. It just got worse.'

Dave introduced Māwera to one of his mates, Graham. Māwera tells it this way: 'I said, "Look, I really need to have a fella in my life. If you don't want to be my fella, I need a fella," so he introduced me to Graham. Graham was quite keen and I think that must've sparked a thing and started changing his thinking. I'm sure that that's what did it.' She looks at Dave for confirmation. 'You don't agree?' Not entirely convincingly, Dave dismisses this as 'women's talk'.

Māwera didn't want to go out with Graham. 'I just wanted to stay with Dave, and I loved his children and I knew they loved me, and we had a family in almost every sense of the word, apart from ... We weren't *together*. But we did everything together. Everyone assumed we were together, but we weren't.'

A year went by. Imagine that, right? A year of flatting with the man you are in love with — a man who is determined not to get into another relationship. A year of cooking, and housekeeping, and childcare, and advocacy — all of which she loved; but she also loved *him*.

David: She made herself irreplaceable, right? She made herself—

Māwera: Indispensable.

David: Indispensable —

Māwera: I did.

David: — is the word, yeah.

By November of 2006, Māwera might have been indispensable, but she was also lonely. 'I got really sad and I said to him, "I'm going to go to the doctor to get antidepressants." He said, "The doctor's never going to give you antidepressants." I said, "Well I'm very sad."

'Anyways, I talked to the doctor and told him I needed antidepressants. He said, "What the hell for?" I told him the whole thing, and he said, "Oh, I thought you were together", because we were always taking the children places together. I said, "No, we're not." Then he said, "I know what: I'm going to give you a prescription for Viagra. I want you to take it home, grind it up, put it in his mashed potatoes and start talking dirty." I cracked up laughing, and he said, "See, you don't need antidepressants. Go home and get him drunk."'

'Which is exactly what she did,' Dave confirms. There was a beautiful dinner — crayfish, possibly, hard to say because there were also three bottles of red wine and some karaoke, and a tiny nightie, and a visit to his room with a glass of water he might have wanted later. He followed her back to her room and ... 'That was that.' By Christmas, they'd moved his stuff into her room.

'Viagra Day', as Māwera and Dave call it, was 16 November 2006 — though I'd like to point out to the Medical Council, and anyone else getting weird ideas, that no prescription was written and there was no actual Viagra in the mashed spuds nor anywhere else: the wine and the lingerie and whatever Māwera cooked for dinner did the trick.

On 5 September 2007, they exchanged promises to each other 'without any pomp or ceremony'. Neither of them want to 'freaking get married' ever again, which leads them both into a vibrant discussion about the history of the institution of marriage, about which they agree on very little except to say that it's not for them. They'll argue about theoretical issues — like whether marriage is a post-industrial concept or not, and Māwera will say something like, 'I wrote a paper on it when I studied anthropology,' and Dave will say, 'Still doesn't mean it's true.' And she'll correct him if he says 'expecially' instead of 'especially', or 'plutonic' when he means 'platonic', but they don't argue about the big stuff.

'We don't argue about things that are fundamental to our life, because we are absolutely on the same page,' Māwera says. 'There's nothing to argue about: we love how we live. He lets me make all the decisions, and then, if he ever overturns a decision, I generally will listen because it means it's something really important. Because otherwise he doesn't bother himself.'

David: You have to listen then, because I don't step in very often.

Māwera: No, he doesn't. He lets me run things. If he steps in, I go, 'Oh shit, something must be horribly wrong with the decision I've made.'

David: Even when I step in sometimes, she doesn't listen.

Māwera: No, mostly I still don't listen.

David: She doesn't listen.

Māwera: [*laughing*] It seems to work well for us.

Over the next 10 years, Māwera focused on raising the kids and finishing her own education. Encouraged by her, Dave tossed in the job he'd stopped enjoying and focused on what he loved — hunting and fishing — making a living out of guiding in summer, plus clearing farmland of avian pests and hunting wild meat. Together, they've built businesses in guided hunting and fishing, and as major suppliers of hand-plucked pheasant and peacock feathers.

And there is something else they've created together — their son, Jack — and it's another homage to persistence, with a sprinkling of remarkable luck. Dave had said to her, albeit drunkenly on Viagra Night, 'We should have a baby.' Māwera had had her tubes tied years earlier, so she knew this was going to be difficult, but she is nothing if not persistent, am I right? She went back to her fabulous GP, who sent her to a gynaecologist. The gynaecologist initially referred her for IVF, but they discovered she was young enough to try for a reversal of the tubal ligation instead. The problem was that they didn't do those in New Zealand, and it would cost $10,000 to have it done in Australia, and they weren't plucking enough pheasants to cover that.

Three months later, the gynaecologist phones to say there is an American specialist in this kind of procedure who just happens to be heading to Whakatāne soon — would Māwera like to see him? Yes, yes she would. During the consultation, Māwera notices he has a fly-fishing rod leaning against the wall. She tells the specialist (whose name is also David) about her own trout-fishing-guide-David. He agrees to do her surgery, and asks whether next Tuesday would be okay. She says she can clear her schedule, sure, but how much will it cost? To which he replies: 'How about your husband takes me fishing and we'll call it even?'

Major surgery with micro stitches. It failed on the first fallopian tube, but succeeded on the other. The men went fishing. Māwera and Dave tried for a year to get pregnant, but no cigar. Next, the GP calls her back in for another procedure, aimed at clearing and widening the re-opened tube. Dave is off hunting, so Māwera asks their mutual friend, Brent, to come along and hold her hand. Brent is a lawyer, and gay. Māwera is assuming the procedure involves an abdominal injection, but it turns out it's a vaginal insertion. When Matthew, the radiologist, sees Brent standing by to support her in the clinic, he says, 'You must be Māwera's husband.' 'No,' Brent says, no doubt discombobulated by what he is about to witness, 'I'm her lawyer.' It took a moment for everyone's blood pressure to return to normal.

Again, the procedure is a success and the scan now shows a properly functioning fallopian tube. Four months later, David-the-American-specialist is back in Whakatāne and asks to see Māwera. 'I walked into his office and sat down and he said, "Right, there are some more things that we can do." I said, "Well, why bother?" He said, "Because you want to have a baby," and I said, "I'm pregnant." He jumped up, lifted me up out of my chair — that's no easy thing to accomplish, either — and he was so excited. A few months after that, I called the midwife and made a little bed on the floor and out popped Jack.'

Māwera tells the tale this time, but it is one Dave loves, and one he has started being the storyteller for. ('It's only when you tell it and they walk away, and then I tell them the real story,' he mutters, mountain-mannishly.) They've all become friends — something special for Doctor David, because he doesn't usually get to watch the kids he's had a hand in creating grow up. Dave likes to introduce him at barbecues with, 'This is David — he got Māwera pregnant.'

And that's how the pheasant-plucker's son was born in November 2009 — precisely three years and one day after Viagra Night. Dave hasn't cut his hair or shaved his beard since — not for any reason he can articulate, but you get a sense it has something to do with relaxing, finally, into being himself.

Neither Dave nor Māwera thinks of themselves as romantic, but they both freely credit each other with creating a life they love. Love, they say, isn't a 'say' word, it's a 'do' word. 'He is my hunter and my fisherman and my gardener. He keeps us fed and happy. It's a good life we have. It's a happy life. We've got a big circle of friends. People come to us generally, because this is where the food is. It's kind of cool.'

Part of their deal is that Māwera doesn't go hunting and fishing with Dave anymore. That's reserved for mates, and it's a long time since they've been 'plutonic' mates. With the businesses and the advocacy and the kids, they could end up spending too much time in each other's company. If he gets on her nerves, she'll say 'Go and kill something' and drop him off at the river. Words to live by.

CHAPTER 13

Sometimes, It's Not Complicated

I DON'T WANT YOU to think the road from meeting to mating is always full of twists and turns. Not every story heads down a cul-de-sac before getting back on the highway, and some couples completely avoid even a hint of catching their undercarriage on a speedbump, or flipping wholly upside-down in a ditch. Because sometimes it really isn't complicated. Life might be, but love isn't.

*

Back in 1964, **Deryn** was 21 years old and living in London. This wasn't your typical backpacking OE: Deryn was widowed (there had been a car accident in the middle of the Tunisian desert, but that's another story), and she had a three-year-old son and a two-year-old daughter.

Deryn says she had left school at 15 years old with nothing but a handful of O Levels, so was somewhat ill-prepared for being a breadwinner. 'Some sort of job training was required, so I enrolled for a course at a place called West London College of Further Education.' It was an old Victorian school in Greyhound Road, and as grim physically as those words together in a sentence might suggest.

Deryn's course was grandly titled 'Ordinary National Diploma in Business Studies', but was, she says, really just a souped-up two-year secretarial course with some languages thrown in. 'I started in September of 1964, and enjoyed it — the children were in full-time day care, and I was amongst a group mostly of school-leavers, but they were an eccentric, kind and interesting bunch. Short forms (in shorthand) were my speciality. And although I'd studied French at my London school, Italian was new and lovely. I got through the first year fine.'

In September 1965, she returned for her second year. 'In the first year, the Italian teacher was Amedeo; in the second year, it was a young guy with a First from Cambridge, fresh back from living some years in Italy, called **David Groves**. He called me "Signora" very respectfully (everybody else was "Signorina" or "Signore") and I could sense some chord being struck somewhere in me.'

Which is a lovely way of expressing that sensation when you meet someone and know they are important, right? The impression of music and harmony and *vibration* somewhere deep within yourself, as though you have always been capable of making this sound, but it took someone else to bring it out of you. An instrument waiting for the right musician.

'David was a sort of erstwhile violinist, and started a little group to play together. I was keen! I could play Handel and Mozart slow movements on the piano, so I joined in. And so it started ...'

These days, lecturers aren't encouraged to have liaisons with students, but 50 years ago it raised no eyebrows whatsoever. Besides, there were only three years between them.

'David was pretty hard-up, and was living in a room down the road from the college with a gas ring and a frying pan under the bed, and drove a little Austin-something ... I lived in a garden flat in Hampstead, and drove a new Volkswagen thanks to a generous mother-in-law. I dressed in olive-green leather (you get the picture), so all in all he regarded me as pretty classy. When he visited my flat for the first time, the row of little shoes outside the door gave him pause to think. It was a very visual reminder of what he was getting into.'

But he did get into it, and so did she. They walked on Hampstead Heath that autumn. 'I was eating an apple at great length, he was waiting until I'd finished, and then he kissed me.' David was 28 and Deryn was 25 when they married in 1967.

Fifty years later, just home from a world trip to celebrate their golden wedding anniversary, I ask Deryn what her name was when she met David Groves. She tells me her maiden name was Brooke-White, and her first married name was Walker. Which has made their family 'a nice mix of Walkers and Groves'. They live now in the paradise that is Paekakariki, Deryn says. 'Happy.'

CHAPTER 14

When Love Makes You Do Crazy Things

THAT SPECTACULAR FRISSON — a sudden moment of 'knowing' — is described so often (not just in this book, but in the story of humanity) that most of us accept it as a rational phenomenon. If a job application asked …

> Q: In which of the following do you believe:
>
> (a) Chemtrails (biological weapons used for mind control)?
>
> (b) Lizard People (all politicians)?
>
> (c) Aliens (probing us)?
>
> (d) Love at first sight?
>
> (e) Bigfoot?

... and you answered (d), you would still get an interview. (You might also get away with (b), given the way things are panning out these days.)

So we don't think of instantly falling in love as 'crazy', but it sure can make you do crazy things. Something risky, or wildly out of character — shagging in the shower block, for example. Or, in this chapter, burgling a boat, or moving to a country you couldn't even pinpoint on a world map.

*

Dominique says **John** fell in love with her tomatoes first. He was from Melbourne; she was from Paris; the tomatoes were from the Occitanie region in southern France.

Born in 1953, Dominique Davaux was raised in the Parisian region, but by 1979, aged 26, she was living in the tiny town of Bourg-de-Visa down in the south-west with her baby daughter. Her previous partner had skipped off to travel the world while Dominique was still pregnant. She practised yoga and self-sufficiency, turning herself into a keen gardener by reading books on how to grow organic vegetables.

'Arwen was seven months old that October,' Dominique says, and then with charming French-to-English phrasing adds, 'We had gone on holidays with friends on the seaside.'

Dominique had told her yoga teacher, Martin, to help himself to her garden while she was away.

Martin is the catalyst here. If you believe that sometimes the Fates arrange one meeting to make another happen, you might picture Martin as their emissary. He had moved into a nearby hamlet and was teaching classes near the house Dominique was renting. Before this, he'd studied yoga in India at an institute in Kerala. It was there that he'd met John Guthrie, another yogi, and they'd become friends, but, before leaving Kerala, they hadn't swapped contact details. Which would mean they'd likely never see each other again, right? Big country, India. Quite a few people. And yet — not once, but twice — they bumped into each other in crowded hot-spots. Finally, Martin gave John his address in France, and told him to swing by if he was ever in the neighbourhood.

And indeed, after visiting England and the Orkney Islands, John made his way to Bourg-de-Visa that October, and went along with Martin to forage in Dominique's garden where he fell in love with *ses tomates biologiques*.

In November, when she and Arwen returned from their holiday, Dominique resumed her yoga classes. 'That fateful evening, I arrived late after settling down my baby. The room was in semi-darkness. I sat down and immediately felt an electric current along my arm, quite a shock. I looked suspiciously on that side and noticed the outline of an unknown person. After the class, all the participants used to come down in the kitchen and share a *tisane*. That is when I was introduced to John.'

His presence in the dimly lit yoga class had sparked (literally) Dominque's attention, but it was about how he *felt* next to her, not about how he looked. In fact over cups of herbal tea, post-yoga, Dominique didn't think he looked all that special, apart from being blond, which was not all that common in the south of France. He was thin — he'd lost weight after contracting hepatitis on his travels — and he felt the cold dreadfully after spending three years in Asia, and months before that working up in Darwin.

'He took the habit of coming to visit me, and he was so helpful, comparing to my other French guy friends,' she says with that endearing French-to-English lilt. And then, making it sound simple, she adds, 'We fell in love.' The complicated bit was that he was about to go back to Australia. 'After three weeks, I asked him if I could come with him to Australia, even though I had no idea where it was.'

Okay, stop the clocks and let's unpack this a little bit. This is not a footloose, flibbertigibbet teenager — this is a 26-year-old woman with a baby, who is a self-sufficient, self-taught organic gardener, talking about moving to a country which is (quite possibly, she's not sure) on the other side of the world to be with someone she has known less than a month. This is not how people usually do things. It is not even how Dominique has usually done things. It is a little crazy.

But they did the crazy thing in a very practical way. 'We were put in touch with people in our district who had worked at the Australian Embassy, and they helped me to get my papers sorted. We had to marry for that: by the mayor of Bourg-de-Visa, with all our friends. A fairly hippy wedding. I never even thought to invite my family. I must have been a quiet rebel?' Dominique says, as though she's still working that out. 'For years we told people that we had married for the Embassy, because we didn't really believe in marriage. We never wore a ring on our left finger.' She says this in a way that implies that, actually, they really liked getting married.

The three of them arrived in Melbourne in May 1980. Dominique hated it. 'The landscape threw me in a despairing state. I was desolate. I could not "understand" the eucalyptus and, that first summer, I could not understand the searing 42-plus degrees heat.' As it happened, John couldn't settle back into Australia either, so they tried New Zealand for milder climes. New Zealand also didn't entirely make sense: Dominique couldn't 'understand' the lack of castles and stone villages, for example. For years she kept herself immersed in French literature, art and history as a kind of salve for homesickness.

But they stayed, and they stayed happy together. They had a son in 1983, and for 20 years they ran a business as biodynamic market gardeners in South Canterbury; they sold it in 2004. John teaches yoga, and Dominique worked for a while as a teacher's aide. 'We are still together after many hardships and upheavals. We live in Waimate.' And, she says, 'We actually still love each other.'

*

Each year when **Faye** and **Warren** celebrate their anniversary — 4 September 1986 — they are celebrating a criminal offence. Don't freak out: they did it politely, and they've managed in the three decades since to avoid a full-on life of crime. Though not before committing at least one other unlawful act. That they'll admit to.

Faye is a teacher, Warren is a financial adviser. They have two perfectly well-adjusted grown-up children, one grandchild, and no mortgage. You would probably meet someone a lot like Faye at a book club (she'd be the fun one), and if you've ever been to a business conference, you've probably sat next to someone like Warren and thought, 'What a good bastard — smart, and funny.' If there's still a tiny part of you that's shocked about them having a criminal past, let me say two things: (1)

so are they, and (2) they were never caught, so I'm not sure that officially they're villains. Just a couple of kids, crazy in love.

Back in 1986, when Faye was 22 years old, she left Wellington to head off on her OE. The goal was Canada, but she stopped in Melbourne first to stay with a friend and earn a bit of coin working in a sandwich bar. Warren — two years older — was one of the flatmates. 'There he was,' she says. 'It was love at first sight for me.' Warren says, yes, there was definitely something there, even though they spent the next couple of weeks 'pretending we weren't interested in each other'. Faye had left a boyfriend at home whom she 'quite liked'; Warren was excruciatingly shy. Still, he'd find excuses to come downstairs around the time Faye was due home from work and hover around the kitchen doing dishes in the hope of bumping into her. Faye thought maybe he was just obsessively tidy.

'And then I pierced your ear,' Faye says — old-school style with a needle, an ice cube and whisky. 'Yeah, and plaited my hair,' Warren adds, which sets Faye off into a reminiscence about his beautiful long hair and the groovy cardigans he sported mid-80s, and her mild disappointment that it gave way to something more Hallenstein-ish later. Hair-plaiting, I suggest, is quite an intimate thing to do for a couple of new flatmates. 'So is piercing the ear,' Warren says. 'Sort of ... symbolic.' Tag and release, I think he means. But not entirely released ...

There's a movie Faye wants to see; she mentions it casually. Warren tells her that he was planning to see something else — would she maybe like to come along? It turned out to be *Stalker*, a Russian art-house movie. 'It's about — what? — three-and-a-half hours long, and *nothing* happens,' Faye says. 'I didn't understand any of it. I was just thinking, "Oh, my God, I don't understand what's going on and this guy is going to ask me questions and talk about it afterwards and I'm not going to know what to say. He's going to think I'm thick because I don't know what the fuck is happening." All I remember is a lot of dripping water and long stares and long shots.'

'I thought it was a good movie,' Warren says. And for the record, he is right. It was the 1979 Soviet sci-fi art film directed by Andrei Tarkovsky. ('Tarkovsky's finest work' — *The Guardian*; 'Tarkovsky is the greatest of them all' — Ingmar Bergman.) It runs at a mere *two*-and-a-half hours. I've watched the trailer. There is indeed a lot of dripping water and long stares and long shots.

A strange first date, Faye says. Coincidentally, she has a work colleague who took a woman to *Stalker*, too, but he never saw her again. 'No, you wouldn't,' Faye says emphatically. 'You *wouldn't* see her again, after that.' They, however, survived — they had a bottle of whisky with them, so no doubt that helped. Afterwards, they caught a tram to St Kilda and sat on the beach, talking. Good chats — possibly not about the movie — until they suddenly realised they'd missed the last tram home. They thought about sleeping on the beach, and then spotted the marina filled with boats they might explore. The marina was gated, but there was a wall that looked scalable. 'I remember,' Warren says, 'you went over the wall first, and I was looking up and I was thinking, "Oh well, if I get arrested it'll be worth it." I followed you over.' Just as they dropped down on the other side, a car drove up to the gates which opened automatically — if they'd waited a few moments, they might have been able to *walk* in. But that wouldn't have been nearly as much fun.

For a while, they lay down on the deck of a boat, watched the waves, gazed at the stars. They still weren't touching. It started to get cold, so, on the off-chance, they tried the hatch. It was unlocked. 'We went down into this beautiful space — luxurious, like a hotel — with a bar!' Faye says. They sat at the bar, poured some more drinks. Everything was, as Goldilocks would say, just right. And then, like Goldilocks, they found a bed, and that was just right, too. From the cabin window, they could see a police launch rocking benignly nearby. They stayed until dawn and then made their getaway — back to their flat, where they both rang in sick and spent the day in bed together. Before they disembarked, they'd tidied up and made the bed in the hope that no one would notice they'd been there.

'Looking back on it, it was a little bit terrible, but ...' Warren says, half shamefaced, half delighted by it all. Faye is a little more convincing: 'Imagine the people coming back and saying, "Who's been having sex in our bed?! It's disgusting!"' And then Faye has a whole conversation with the two versions of herself: the wild, falling-in-love, carefree young woman, and the mature, responsible woman she is now. 'For me, I think about the story as exciting and fun, but then I think about the people who owned the boat, and I think, as an older person, that it's just an invasion of someone else's property.' She means it, but she's also laughing as she says this. 'It's actually an offence!' Did she think about that at all at the time? 'No! It wouldn't even have occurred to me. In our twenties, we thought we owned the whole world. It was ours.'

For his part, Warren says he *did* realise at the time that it wasn't really a very good idea. 'I didn't care about the people; I just cared about getting caught. But it was worth the risk.'

I tell them I still don't care about the boat-owners. 'If I owned a boat that had a bar in it,' I say with all the confidence of someone who has never owned a boat with a bar in it and never will, 'I would hope that people like you would turn up and fall in love on it. And if I didn't feel like that, I would have a little chat with myself about my lack of generosity.'

It's a story they tell at dinner parties — Faye usually as raconteur, Warren enjoying the audience response. Faye says recalling themselves as adventurous young risk-takers is a positive thing for them as they get older and (she is laughing as she says this) less adventurous. And it's a significant story, Warren says, because it represents the flavour of their relationship at the time. 'That's how I remember it. Our relationship at the beginning was exciting and was a bit on the edge.'

Faye agrees they had been up for anything, and then drops this into the conversation: 'We took risks, like ... We had sex in an art gallery.' We spend a few minutes clarifying this — upstairs in a café above a gallery. Faye says the café was open, Warren insists it had closed for the day; Faye points out anyone could still have walked in, which made it very exciting. So we're not talking a table-ending in front of a visiting exhibition of Renaissance art at two in the afternoon while school children are visiting, but it's admirable all the same.

'That was what I've liked about Faye. I thought she was exciting. It felt a bit sort of Bonnie-and-Clyde, that *romance*. We weren't really outlaws, we were just middle-class kids. But we thought we were Bonnie and Clyde.'

Thirty years down the track, they're enjoying a longer and happier ending than Mr Barrow and Ms Parker, but it wasn't a foregone conclusion. The day after they burgled the boat,

Faye says Warren told her that due to a previous heartbreak he could never really love again. He has absolutely no recollection of saying any such thing, but it's evident from the sighing and eye-rolling from him as she recounts this that he's quite familiar with her version of this story. What he will say is that it took him longer to work out they were in this thing for the long haul.

The following conversation is punctuated with much laughter:

Warren: I thought it would last a year, and then after a year I thought maybe five years. That's max. Then it was five years and we'd had a child by then, I think. Did we?

Faye: Yeah, but you never wanted children.

Warren: That's another thing I don't remember.

Faye: You did not want children. I left you when I was 23, because I felt I was getting old and I'd have to go and find someone else, because I was running out of time.

Me: Yeah, well, ovaries. Twenty-three, you're just about — They're poached.

Faye: I know. So I left him for a couple of days. Do you remember that?

Warren: No. No, I don't. I've heard this story a lot, but I don't actually recall it ... So anyway, after about 15 years I thought maybe, I don't know, this is probably serious.

And we talk about my 15-year theory: that if you survive that long, you stop asking whether you should be together, and focus on *being* together. Faye says heaven knows how they managed the first 15 — that she used to be 'difficult' — but she isn't anymore. 'But there was never any doubt,' Warren says, 'even through the bad times, that we loved each other.'

Their children were born in 1990 and 1993, and love hearing about the night their sensible, decent parents broke into the marina at St Kilda and helped themselves to someone's floating bar. Not traditionally 'romantic' (they joke with each other about how not-romantic they are), there was never a wedding, but they love to celebrate, so 4 September is marked each year. Faye says the best year was when Warren cooked a full degustation and she read her book between courses. 'That was just fabulous.'

I suggest that one year on their anniversary they should re-enact the fateful night and break into a boat somewhere. Warren sensibly points out that everything's monitored these days with security cameras and alarms. Hire the boat, I tell them, and just pretend to break in. Peals of laughter from Faye. 'We should do it,' she says, 'we really should.' Honestly, I reckon they're still up for anything. It's either that or a visit to an art gallery.

*

There is another story about an outrageous risk a young couple took, throwing caution — and propriety — to the wind almost 90 years ago, but we are saving that for later. Right now, I want to understand more about this 'love at first sight' business — the sudden knowing, an electric shock, a chord being struck. What is it that attracts us to someone? And what is going on that makes you — if not officially crazy — not quite yourself? Let's go visit your brain again.

CHAPTER 15

The Science of Attraction

ASK PEOPLE WHO HAVE been together for an eon, or part thereof, what they find attractive about their One In Particular, and they will make lists of things they appreciate about each other and stuff they have in common. They'll tell you that they share the same values and similar politics; enjoy the same variety (and volume) of food and wine; have matching tastes in books and movies and music; admire each other's work ethic or bathroom etiquette. Or they'll describe how they dovetail — he cooks, she likes to eat; she's a whiz at five-year plans, he's adept at getting shit done at the weekend.

But these are things you discover in the days and decades after you've met. What about the instant stuff that happens in those first few seconds before you've seen their bookshelves? Before you know if they like spicy food, what they do with wet towels, how they feel about pay equity? What makes you want to throw your lot in with someone you've just met and run off to Australia? At the risk of dissecting the love-frog — and ending up with nothing more than a steaming pile of entrails and a dead frog — let's take a look at how two people might immediately start fancying each other like two prairie voles on heat.

The human spirit is a complex thing that can't entirely be measured by science but, happily, that doesn't stop scientists having a jolly good crack at it. The generally accepted theory is that romantic and sexual attraction is all about the kids: we are drawn to other humans who look like they'd help us make good babies. So we are attracted to people who appear healthy and strong enough to birth or protect our young. We are so hardwired with this that it doesn't even matter if we currently (or ever) want to make actual babies. It's worth noting that we've only had access to a relatively reliable form of birth control since the 1960s — maybe we'll evolve past this 'making babies' default position in time, but we might have to give it a minute.

We can spot strong genes and good health from a fair distance. Some of it is to do with 'symmetry' and 'averageness'. Symmetry just means one side of your face matches the other side (we tend to judge people with highly symmetrical faces as 'beautiful' because we understand instinctively that it indicates genetic fitness); but 'averageness' goes a little deeper. It seems that on any given day as we go about our business, we make a mental note of all the faces we see. By dinner time, our brain has compiled a composite of all those faces and it tells us, 'This is what, on average, people should look like.' Which is why, if you get off a plane in a different country, at first you notice how different everyone looks. Spend enough time there, and when you go home you will find that your friends and neighbours look odd. On an unconscious level, our brain is encouraging us to stick with members of our own tribe — or at least to immediately notice someone who might be from a different tribe, thereby alerting us to check whether they are friend or foe. Makes sense historically, right? 'You don't look like you're from around here' was once a very useful thing to be able to say if you lived in a village constantly under threat from marauding strangers. Not quite such a life-and-death issue once you're making a fair portion of your GDP out of international tourism. But, like I say, evolution takes time.

There are other tiny things we read unconsciously — the limbal ring, for example, that dark line some people have around the iris where it meets the whites of your eyes, which signals youth and health. And we can get super-technical with the 'Golden Ratio': ideally, you want the distance between your eyes and mouth to be about 36 per cent of the length of your face, and the distance between your eyes should be 46 per cent of your face's width. Nah, don't get your ruler out — you will know if you do or don't fit the Golden Ratio instinctively, just by knowing whether you look better with your hair pulled back, or with a fringe.

The theory goes that this general stuff is true for both men and women, gay and straight. Some or all of which will be making you say 'bollocks' around about now. 'I love someone who doesn't look anything like me or mine', or 'I am attracted to maturity, not youth', or 'I fell in love with someone who has a really wonky face'. That's because, scientists theorise, we also have our own individual 'love map'. 'Love map' is a decidedly unscientific term, but you've got to get your funding from somewhere, so possibly science-y people think up phrases like this so their research gets quoted in articles that might have a chance of being picked up by the *Huffington Post*.

Anyhoo, you draw your own 'love map' based on personal taste and experiences. People raised by older parents, for example, are less likely to be wowed by the beauty of youth: if the first people you loved and trusted were older, you may be more open to loving and trusting someone with a less youthful face. Plus there will be myriad things you do or don't like for whatever reason — tattoos, uniforms, ample bosoms, hairy chests, brunettes, vivacious laughs — it's your map, and you can put anything on it you want. Fill your boots.

Some people's love map is so specific that they can end up having a discernible 'type'. I have a friend who seems to have only ever dated one woman, but really, over the years, there have been several of them who just look remarkably the same. 'Lovely to see you again!' I'll chirrup when we meet up in the pub, and she's bewildered and everyone is uncomfortable while I work out she's not the one who came with him for drinks the last time. This is a new one. Awkward.

Hardwired, then, for reproduction, and with love map in hand, in those first few seconds of clapping eyes on someone a whole bunch of information is being communicated below the level of consciousness. You're not aware of ticking off a shopping list, although you might register some parts of it specifically: 'What I first noticed was his eyes.' But you are unlikely to be thinking, 'My word, that is a very bold limbal ring.' Though, now that I've mentioned it, you might give that a try, yes?

And then there are the things we are looking for which are specific to our gender and sexual orientation. Let's talk about straight men first, because that's what we usually do. Visually, what they find attractive in a woman (run with me, we can argue later) are childbearing hips, plus small chins and less prominent brows, all of which indicate higher levels of oestrogen and fertility. Always with the baby-making, bless you, Mother Nature.

(Quick side note: some recent studies show that men who are hungry are more likely to be attracted to women who look well fed — they're hardwired to spot women who appear to have access to plentiful food sources. Dieting is stupid for so many reasons, and there's another one. All we really need to do is hang around outside restaurants and be our charming voluptuous selves before they get a chance to go inside and eat. Apparently, they also find us pretty when we smile. Chuck that in as well, if you need to.)

In those first few seconds of meeting, we are not just *seeing* — we are hearing and smelling, too. A small example is that straight men are traditionally thought to be attracted to women with higher-pitched voices. And wouldn't you know it, there is evidence that straight women automatically speak in a higher pitch when they're attracted to the man they are talking to. Jeepers, we're clever.

But wait, there's more. Let me tell you about the incredible powers of straight men. It's not restricted to running corporations and governments, ladies — there are other things they can do. Like, they can actually *smell* when you are ovulating and therefore at your most fertile, and *see* it in your face, and *hear* it in your voice. Bloody hell. It's a skill they picked up back in caveman times before dating was a thing (it is a thing, right?), which enabled them to quickly identify the woman in the cave most likely to get pregnant on any given day, and therefore take the opportunity to make it so. Tough times in the caves: short life expectancy, killer mammoths, and an innate drive to ensure the survival of the species. A man had to do what a man had to … et cetera.

There is general agreement that this ability to *smell* ovulation is likely due to pheromones, those scent-bearing chemicals secreted in sweat and other bodily fluids. Animals rely on them because they can't chat or go to the movies, but we use them, too. Which is not a reason to stop chatting or going to movies, but this is seriously fascinating, right? Just so that we're all on the same page, let's note that women are fertile on the day of ovulation and for the five days before that. For the average woman (albeit that there is no such thing as an average woman) that means somewhere between days 10 and 17. It seems that right there in the middle part of her 28-day menstrual cycle, a woman exudes pheromones that make her more attractive to men. They know this because, at the University of Texas, they gave men a pile of women's T-shirts to sniff. Some had been worn while the women were ovulating, some were worn when they weren't. The men judged the T-shirts the women wore when they were fertile as smelling more 'pleasant' and 'sexy'.

What is even more extraordinary is that men don't even have to sniff a T-shirt to know. They can just see it in her face.

Not only in her real-life face — in a *picture* of her face, too. There was a British study that asked men to look at photos of women and rate their attractiveness. (Like a Tinder-based science experiment.) The first bunch of photos were taken when the women weren't ovulating. Some days later, they were shown photos of the same women, but the photos had been taken when they *were* ovulating, and the men consistently judged them this time as more attractive. The lesson here? Take your Tinder profile photo when you're ovulating, not when you've got your period.

Smell it and see it, and also *hear* ovulation. By which I'm not suggesting men can pick up the sound of an egg dropping out of a fallopian tube — *kerplunk* — but it seems that ovulation changes the tone of your voice in a way that men love. There is evidence that, at peak fertility, a woman's voice can literally make a man's skin tingle.

All of this is about Mother Nature getting him and her together at the optimum time for baby-making. The woman he most fancies in the room is the one who is most likely to get pregnant that day. Which might mean that, in terms of safe sex, you should never shag the woman you find most attractive on any given night in a bar. Go for someone you fancy a bit, but not heaps, in the same way you might pick the second cheapest bottle of wine on the menu. Though this is a terrible idea, and I am sorry I mentioned it. Follow your heart and use a condom.

As much as we might be gobsmacked by a man's ability to see, smell and hear when a woman is fertile, women have — drumroll please — equivalent superpowers, used for a slightly different purpose. From about three metres away, some scientists suggest, she can smell his immune system. Immune system! Which was terrifically useful for a cavewoman wanting to ensure that he will (a) pass on good genes and (b) survive long enough to provide and protect. Not only this, women can also smell how symmetrical a man's face is before they even see it. I kid you not. It's the T-shirt test again: women were asked to smell men's sweaty singlets and, just from a quick whiff, they could pick which ones belonged to the most symmetrical (and therefore virile and healthy) men. Seriously, no one needs to turn the lights on, ever.

When it comes to what women look for visually, however, we may already be in the early years of evolutionary change. The traditional theory was that women prefer more masculine-looking men — the markers of masculinity being broad shoulders as a sign of good health and strength; a prominent brow and strong jaw formed by high testosterone, indicating virility; and facial hair — stubble when we are looking for sex, full beard when we're looking for mature fathering potential.

But it seems this doesn't hold true anymore, certainly not in the developed world. So much has changed for women in recent decades — we have careers, financial self-sufficiency, so much independence that wc can actually survive without a mate — that it is possible we may be evolving to look for other things. A pal, an intellectual equal, some gentleness and kindness. There is a theory that women are hot right now for more 'feminine-looking' men. Ryan Gosling, Brad Pitt, Bradley Cooper, Johnny Depp ... as opposed to Richard Burton, Clark Gable, Cary Grant, Gregory Peck. Except — and this could be tricky if it's true — that might change briefly when you're in the fertile part of your cycle and the old drive for a manly-man raises its head. You might be married to Orlando Bloom but, when you're ovulating, fancy Chris Hemsworth. Disaster. (Though I reckon Chris has quite lady-lovely eyes.) I'm not sure where Benedict Cumberbatch fits in all this, except to say he looks like a very sexy otter, gender-fluid. Which, when you think about it, would work all month.

So our evolving social structure might be causing a small shift in what straight women find 'attractive'. Big, beefy boys — out; friendly and thoughtful nerds — in. I'm exaggerating, obviously, but only because I think it helps.

And then there's 'The Pill Effect': biochemical changes brought about by the oral contraceptive, available since the early 1960s. Traditionally, women have been instinctively drawn to men whose major histocompatibilty complex (MHC) genes are different from her own — mating outside your gene pool makes the kids healthier, with better immune systems. But there is some evidence that when women are on the Pill, they are attracted instead to men whose MHC is similar to their own. The theory is that the hormonal changes in pregnancy (which the Pill mimics) draw women to 'nurturing relatives' rather than 'strangers / potential baby-daddies'. If this is true — it's still in the theory stage — it is potentially hazardous. You're on the Pill (good woman, very responsible); you fall in love with someone with a similar MHC; you decide to start a family (big step, make sure you talk it through) and go off the Pill, and — *bam!* — suddenly you're looking at someone who feels like a brother to you rather than a lover. On the upside, if you manage to get over that hump and get pregnant, you will be thrilled with him and his similar MHCs again, recognising instantly that he is exactly the right person for fetching pickles and ice cream, and for giving foot rubs. Well done, you.

While lots of this attraction theory seems overwhelmingly primal and therefore out of your control, there are aspects you absolutely do have influence over. Like being kind and honest. It's 'the Halo Effect', which has been studied in various experiments, but it generally goes like this: without being aware of it, we judge people who are pleasant and respectful and enthusiastic as being all the other good things — including both intelligent and attractive. (This works both ways: we tend to assume beautiful people are 'good' and ugly people are 'evil', hence the way movies and TV commercials are cast.) Studies suggest that if you show someone a photo of a person and say 'This person is kind and honest' and then ask them to rate their attractiveness, they will say the person has a lovely face. Show the next person the same photo and tell them 'This person is mean and dishonest', and they will judge them a veritable bush-pig. So your behaviour has an impact on how 'good-looking' people think you are. It's an interesting phenomenon, and possibly explains why, during a fight, you might suddenly look at your partner and think, 'Eew, what a dork — what did I ever see in him?' And when you make up, you think, 'Actually? He's quite hot.' Cue make-up-sex.

Less research has been done (of course it has) on the chemistry of gay and lesbian attraction, but it is entirely possible that women who love each other are reading each other's fertility and immune systems, and gay men are attuned to each other's genetic health and virility, because, like all humans, they are looking to create their own family. Certainly the universal things about symmetry and averageness hold true, along with the personalised love map. A Harvard study found that, in general, men — gay or straight — are wired to be attracted to facial features most synonymous with gender. Manly-men and feminine-women score highly on their general 'attractiveness' scorecards, regardless of whether that attraction is 'sexual'. The same study found that lesbians and straight women had slightly different ideas of what 'attractive' was: straight women preferred more masculine-faced men than lesbian women, while lesbians preferred slightly more masculine female faces than either straight women or men. From which we can only conclude that there is *someone* out there who will find each of us absolutely perfectly freaking gorgeous.

That's the thing, right? For all these rules born into us, we break them all the time. People fall in love with narrow-hipped women, weak-jawed men, post-menopausal women with nary a whiff of fertility, people with no discernible limbal ring around eyes that sit in wholly asymmetrical faces. And people fall in love with people who aren't healthy or strong — more than once, a medical professional has fallen in love with a patient, for instance. If they didn't, we wouldn't have so many hospital-based TV dramas for starters. We may have all of these built-in drives that have us searching for the clinically perfect face and body, but none of us is perfect and we still get to fall in love, and have people love us.

But some of this might explain those moments of instant attraction. I don't want to diminish the magic of what

Dominique felt in that yoga class when she sat down in the dark next to John, but maybe she was smelling his immune system. Perhaps Deryn was doing the same when David called her 'Signora' while he was teaching her Italian. It could be that when Warren met Faye in the kitchen, he could hear her ovulate. It is possible Māwera saw Dave's jaw and brow and read his testosterone levels that day when he was surrounded by dead pheasants. And Roger was swept off his feet — either at the top or the bottom of the stairs, we will never know — by Briony's limbal ring, and vice versa. Jane was possibly entirely right when she talked of meeting Tim on the day he was hit by a car, and she put the whole thing down to 'chemicals'.

It might all be science. Or it could all be magic. Or bits of both. The trouble with life, American anthropologist Ruth Benedict once observed, isn't that there is no answer, but that there are *so many* answers. Personally, I'm inclined to agree with French mathematician, physicist and moralist (that's a helluva business card) Blaise Pascal, who said: *'Le coeur a ses raisons que la raison ne connaît point.'* ('The heart has its reasons which reason knows nothing of.') Yet here we are: we have these smelling/hearing/seeing superpowers for a purpose, and you'd be a fool to argue they're not playing some part in how we manage to arrange ourselves as couples.

So these are the scientific theories about love at first sight — and love at first smell, and first sound. But what happens next? How do you get from 'I quite fancy her' to scaling the walls of a marina and breaking into a yacht? It is because, Dear Reader, once you are attracted to someone, your brain turns into a drug dealer.

CHAPTER 16

The Chemistry of Love

YOU'VE JUST MET your wide-hipped, fertile woman with the high-pitched voice, or your virile man with the square and stubbly jaw (or whatever it is you have on your personal love map), and the next thing you know, your mouth is dry, you can't eat or sleep (which is fine, you've somehow got heaps of energy) and the world is a truly wonderful place. Light is brighter, kittens are fluffier, everything feels hopeful and You Can Do Anything. Because you are, in fact, as high as a kite.

Earlier in this book, I asked you to imagine that your brain was an office, filled with file boxes. Now I want you to imagine your brain is a pharmacy, filled with drugs. The good drugs — the fun ones that make you peppy and happy and optimistic. Taking charge of your brain-pharmacy is a very generous dealer, handing out various feel-good comestibles — no prescriptions required, no appointment necessary.

Of course, describing your brain as a drug dealer is, as a

metaphor, entirely around the wrong way. Our brains invented all this mood-altering stuff first. Old Stoney McStoneface, in the tinny house down the road with the sneakers hanging over his powerlines, is, in fact, selling you something that only mimics the chemicals your brain is naturally capable of producing given the right circumstances. Even so, let's imagine your brain is Pablo Escobar, but with a conscience, working pro bono, wanting nothing but the very best for you.

Here's how it goes. Imagine two people experience a mutual attraction. They look into each other's eyes. Immediately, the adaptive oscillators fire up their orbital frontal cortex, which sets off a chemical reaction in each other's brains, and all hell breaks loose. This is a step past the 'Crikey, she looks fertile/he looks virile' individual reaction. This is a shared response triggered by the mutual gaze.

Phase one is Lust — an ocean-surge of oestrogen for women, a tsunami of testosterone for men. Just in case you weren't picking up on each other's pheromones loud and clear, this boost of hormones from Pablo in your brain-pharmacy should have that covered.

Phase two is Attraction. Pablo gives you a decent shot of adrenaline (experienced as sweaty armpits and a dry mouth), which is the human fuel for fight or flight (and clearly another thing that starts with 'f', which might be on the cards if you play them right). Think of adrenaline as 'speed'. Pablo also has dopamine, the naturally produced desire-and-reward chemical which is similar to cocaine. Dopamine is the reason you're not hungry or tired, and can stay up all night talking at great length and in great detail about things you are suddenly very passionate and clear about. You will take delight in small things, and everything brings you pleasure. For good measure, Pablo also gives you a hit of serotonin, a mood stabiliser that deals to any depression or anxiety, and makes everything seem fabulous (including your very own self) in much the same way as MDMA ('ecstasy') does. You're not going to doubt that they adore you at this point — you feel entirely adorable. When you do get around to sleeping, serotonin makes it a peaceful sleep. It also keeps your bowels regular, which is a bonus under any circumstances.

Phase three is Attachment. Like any dealer, Pablo's plan is to get you hooked on each other, so he has some special treats to cement this new addiction. Oxytocin is often called 'the cuddle hormone', and Pablo doles it out liberally at orgasm to encourage you to hang about and get to know each other a little more. It is also Pablo's go-to drug during childbirth (for pain relief, and so women forget labour and focus on the newly delivered human, isn't it cute), and he tops up the oxytocin doses during breastfeeding, too. If you have ever experienced (or witnessed) that roll-your-eyes-back-in-your-head peaceful relaxation that envelops a nursing mother, you will appreciate that Pablo has some really good gear in his pharmacy. And to reinforce the pleasure of cuddling — and make it specific to the *person* you are cuddling rather than just about cuddling in general — he will spot you a good dose of vasopressin. Vasopressin is the natural chemical that bonds you to your partner long term — the 'mate for life' drug. It keeps you wanting to have sex with them regardless of interest in reproduction, but rather as a joyful recreational activity. It is Mother Nature essentially apologising for that 'get together and make babies, quick!' imperative by offering up long-term commitment and friendship via a whole lifetime of fun sexy-times. 'You've made a kid, thanks so much — now do right by each other and enjoy each other's company. Pablo? Give them the vasopressin, stat!'

To work some of this out, neuroscientists and endocrinologists have studied prairie voles — they look a bit like a cross between a guinea pig and a very cute brown mouse. Prairie voles have much more sex than they strictly need to, and they form stable pair-bonds. Please note: those two things are related. Sex-for-the-sake-of-it and long-term-bonding. We know this because when researchers inhibited vasopressin in prairie voles (sounds cruel, why would you do that?), they found that the voles stopped having their just-for-the-pleasure-of-it sex and — this is the critical bit — consequently stopped giving much of a hoot about each other. Mr Vole failed to help with the childcare and didn't bother defending the nest from threats, ceased listening to Ms Vole with her stories about her day, and, before you could say 'couples counselling', started putting it about with other voles, willy-nilly. Like, wow. It's a story from the suburbs. We've all met those vasopressin-suppressed prairie voles. Some of us have been them. Fortunately, all this misery was able to be reversed with a nice big shot of fresh vasopressin, administered in the lab. Please stop worrying about the voles: they're fine now.

What can we learn from Pablo and the prairie voles? (Side note: great name for a band.) That when we fall in love, we are in fact as high as a freaking kite on a cocktail of what would otherwise be some serious Class A drugs — speed, cocaine and ecstasy. Given this, it is not at all surprising that you do crazy things — things you might otherwise think were irrational, or out of character. Not quite yourself? I'll say. You are completely out of your tiny mind. In a lovely way. But, yeah, burgle a boat and have sex in an art gallery? Up sticks and move halfway around the world? Risk getting caught in the showers? Jump on a plane after a midnight phone call? Can't imagine why not. Not in this state. Plus, once you start falling in love, it would be hard to pull yourself out of it — Pablo keeps finding powerful and (literally) mind-altering substances to keep you in that state, leaving you with no desire to give it up. I can't help thinking that this must explain to some extent the 'rebound' relationship — falling *out* of love and very quickly falling *in* love with someone else. You're jonesing for Pablo to re-up his drug supply, particularly those very high 'highs' he's pushing in the Attraction phase.

From the voles, the take-home message would be that we need to pay attention to the Attachment phase if we want to last the distance. Sex for pleasure, and sticking around long enough after said sex for the oxytocin and vasopressin to be released. Long days in bed aren't an indulgence, they are a necessity. Explain this in broad terms to the kids when you plop them in front of the telly on a Saturday morning and lock the bedroom door. 'Mummy and Daddy need to do some pair-bonding.' Find the Nature channel and let them watch some prairie voles. They really are very cute.

One of the things I find endearing about all this drug-induced madness is that the whole chain of events is initiated by something as simple as gazing into someone else's eyes. That's what initially fires up the adaptive oscillators in our orbital frontal cortex. We shouldn't underestimate the power of a bit of eye-gazing; it has other uses, too. There is separate research that shows gazing into the eyes of your dog or cat releases oxytocin in both of you simultaneously, relieving stress and imbuing you both with feelings of love. I'm not a scientist, but I'm thinking if it works with Fluffy and Bouncer, it is also working for you and your human pal. It's one of the things I notice when couples tell their stories together: lots of eye contact with each other rather than with me, and a sense by the end that people might need to get a room. It's worth tucking away in your arsenal of how-to-keep-things-great weaponry. Like they say, falling in love is easy (it's the drugs), but staying in love is hard (so get the drugs where you can). You don't always have time for the full horizontal tango, but there's always time for a loving look. Try to keep Pablo gainfully employed.

*

Under the weight of all this science, I reckon we can agree that attraction can absolutely be instant. A look, a voice, a sniff. But the attraction-to-attachment process doesn't all have to happen in a short space of time. Sometimes, people see someone and nothing happens for years — except that they've been filed away in some corner of your brain-office. Let's find out how delightful it can be when you rediscover them and retrieve that memory later.

CHAPTER 17

Don't I Know You from Somewhere?

IN TERMS OF PLOT, some of the tales I love best are the ones with hidden connections, where two people get together, and then, over months or years, peel back the layers to uncover more stories that involve them both. Patrick and Maria, for example, discovering that their shared narrative began many years before they met. That image of Maria's boss bursting into work one morning, convinced she'd found the perfect man for Maria in a restaurant the night before (and Maria brushing it off) still makes me grin.

She and Patrick hadn't seen each other at the start — there'd been no opportunity to assess each other's fertility or immunity, no reading of symmetry or Golden Ratio, no sniffing, or any kind of love-map navigation. But for some other couples, there has been a moment of 'recognition', a face seen and noted as significant, and filed away until later. Someone you saw on TV, or in a picture, or maybe it involves some rusty old Kiwi number 8 wire. Or you might work out that, years before, he did your hair.

*

In 1980, **Kate McRae** was 15 years old and at home watching the telly. *University Challenge* was on, and the Otago team was winning. This was due in no small part to **Bruce Russell**, a 19-year-old politics student. Kate says she was immediately struck by him because he didn't look like the others. 'He wore a fringed leather jacket and a red beret, and he answered just about every question. Or, at least, that's how I remember it.'

Kate met Bruce in the real world a year later. She was in her first year at Canterbury University, and he was working there part-time. She recognised him instantly as the guy from the TV, but was never brave enough to talk to him. 'He was far too cool.'

'Then, in 1985, I was completing my BA in political studies at Otago Uni and I took a paper in the Philosophy of Karl Marx, and guess who my lecturer was? That's right — him! Nothing "happened" between us, but at least I got to actually meet him that time.'

It was five years later — 1990, and a full 10 years after she'd first laid eyes on him — that they finally got together. 'It turned out we were both living in the same street in Port Chalmers. I remember the day clearly: we literally bumped into each other at a vegie shop. I had just got a speeding ticket and was so mad I had to tell someone, so he got an earful from me. Then later that same afternoon I bumped into him again on the street.'

Kate invited him around to her house, which was up a long path and hidden by trees. 'I was in the process of lifting a raised floor, and there were all these exposed nails everywhere. He offered to come with his hammer and fix it for me. He had me at "hammer", to be honest. I made him tomato soup, and we've been together ever since, and have three wonderful children together.'

They got married two years after Bruce came over to whack the nails in. Bruce now has a PhD, manages the School of Art and Design at Christchurch Polytechnic, and is a musician. Kate is an artist who also bakes for a local café.

'And the answer to the question everyone wants to know when I say I married my lecturer is, yes, he did give me an A.'

*

Let me introduce you now to **Stayci Taylor**. Stayci is going to turn up again in another chapter, too, along with two minor characters from this tale (the 'feral Dunedinites'). Here, though, she stars alongside her partner of more than two decades, **Lucy Schmidt**.

Jeremy and I have both known Lucy and Stayci for a very long time — we've all done theatre and comedy and improv and festivals together at various times — but I'd never heard the story of how they met until we did that thing Kiwis sometimes do: bumped into each other in a foreign country and hooked up for a splendid night out involving, in this case, Aperol Spritz cocktails and *aperitivo* in Florence. That evening, sitting in a square in front of Basilica di Santo Spirito, we swapped stories about what we'd been up to in the years since they'd moved to Melbourne and we hadn't seen them, and I told them about this book. The next day, all I could remember about how they'd met was that it was delightful, and had involved Lucy seeing a picture of Stayci. (As has been noted before, my brain is soluble in alcohol.) Back at home, in much the same way as I'd asked Ian and Clare, my ground-zero couple, to send me a properly accurate version of events, I emailed Lucy and Stayci. They sent not one, but two stories. And here they are.

My partner, Lucy, is not part of the hometown crowd. Even so, all roads, as ever, lead back to Dunedin, where I met the man who would become our mutual bestie. Sean and I left Dunedin around the same time for different theatre schools — mine in Melbourne, his in Wellington, where he considerately invested in befriending my future life partner.

In a nice piece of symmetry, Sean eventually joined me in Melbourne — his hometown — with what was meant to be Lucy in tow, but she kept booking acting work and postponing her departure. I wasn't altogether unhappy with the delay, given this unknown woman seemed to be occupying the position of naughty, funny friend that was usually reserved for me.

As it happened, I first met her on a visit back to New Zealand where, on Sean's instructions, she'd given up her room in Wellington for me and two other feral Dunedinites, relegating both her and her then girlfriend to a very small couch in an already busy Newtown flat. This act of generosity only added to my begrudging realisation she was indeed as clever, talented and funny as Sean kept banging on about.

She would eventually make her way to Melbourne where, as both flatmates and bandmates, we broke the screw-the-crew rule twice over. Sean, having hoped his two ladies would get on, got more than he bargained for.

— Stayci Taylor

I first saw Stayci in a photograph. Our mutual friend, Sean, had been at the Adelaide Festival that year, and was showing me photos of post-show antics. As I flicked through the stack, I saw this intriguing-looking woman, and started to grill him about her. It's weird how drawn to that photograph I was, considering I am now in my twenty-first year as her beloved partner. I remember staring at it for quite some time. I still have it. (Stace doesn't think it even looks like her.)

When I first came to Melbourne, I stayed at her flat. She was always running off to some rehearsal or band practice. In demand, I guess. The intrigue grew. We became friends and drinking buddies — we started a band together with another friend that we still play in to this day. She was the funniest person I'd ever met. I realised I was in love with her one day when she was drumming with her band, The Sharons. She embodied joy. It took me six months of my best behaviour to get her to fall for me. A very good investment as it turned out.

— Lucy Schmidt

'She embodied joy' is possibly the most beautiful, romantic thing anyone has ever said about another person. Closely followed by: 'She was indeed as clever, talented and funny as Sean kept banging on about.'

*

You know the old saying: Marry in haste, peel back the layers at leisure. After a whirlwind romance, **Susan and Russell Smith** have been finding connections between the two of them for more than a quarter of a century now.

'In 1990, Russell moved in as a flatmate with my nine-year-old daughter and me. We fell in love within a week, even though I played hard to get for a few days. We didn't muck around: we invited our combined friends and family to a Christmas party, and Santa turned up and married us. That was so much fun!'

As they got to know each other, they discovered the coincidences. Both had grown up in small towns and moved to Auckland as soon as they could — not an unusual story, right? But wait. Ten years older than Susan, Russell had arrived in Auckland a decade sooner than her. He lived on Crummer Road in Ponsonby, and trained as a hairdresser at a salon on Karangahape Road. Ten years later, when Susan arrived in Auckland, she also lived on Crummer Road and found a job in a cute little boutique in St Kevin's Arcade on Karangahape Road. So matching geographical starts to life in the big city.

There's more. When she was 14, Susan had visited Auckland and stayed with relatives in Te Atatū. 'I had long hair and had saved up to get a trendy cut. I was told that a new salon had started up the road, so I wandered up and this lovely, shy guy gave me an amazing haircut. It turns out it was Russell — though he can't remember me then!'

*

It's a bleak sort of day when I drive south to Hamilton to meet **Sally and Neil Hunter**, but their mobile home is bright and warm, and there is carrot cake. Really good carrot cake, still warm from Sally's oven. Proper cream-cheese icing, laid on thick. They have a house in Kawerau, but they've parked up their fancy house-bus in a Waikato campground to be near their daughter and granddaughter. They've done all kinds of work over the years, including being foster parents and running a family business. Right now, Neil is a crane operator and Sally does volunteer work and helps out around the campground. Her sister died a year earlier, so Sally had stepped away from full-time work to spend time with her when she was ill. Sometimes the mobile home goes to where Neil has work —

he helped build the Novotel in New Plymouth in 2015 — but mostly it stays here, near their grandchild.

Neil and Sally were both born in 1956, and both of them look ridiculously young for their age. It takes me a while to put my finger on it, but Sally reminds me of English actor Geraldine James, who played the sexy redhead in *The Jewel in the Crown* opposite Art Malik back in the 1980s and, more recently, the human female Rebel pilot in *Rogue One: A Star Wars Story.* Stunning long red hair and a shy smile, with a hint of hippie. Neil has a gentle air about him, too, despite the fact he could be the lovechild of Guyon Espiner and that guy who played Toby Ziegler in *The West Wing.* When they met in the 1970s, he had shoulder-length dark waves — Sally says he looked like Donna Summer with a moustache, which all of us find hilarious. She means it in a good way: she fancied him the moment she saw him at a friend's flat in Palmerston North. Possibly chased him a bit. Because she knew, she says, he was The One. Sally's friend was going out with Neil's best friend, and those two had become lovers. Sally wanted to lose her virginity, too, but it had to be more involved than just sex. 'I wanted love, and feelings.' 'It had to be the right person,' Neil says, 'and she got all that.'

This was in 1973 when she was 16, he was 17. Neil had a girlfriend, but that didn't mean he didn't notice Sally. 'I was really attracted to her, because she was quite different with her red hair and her hot-pants up to here,' he says, pointing somewhere around his armpits. 'She was Miss Bulls!' Like literally, crowned and everything, her photo in the local newspaper. 'Miss Bulls ...' Sally says, being entirely self-deprecating about winning this kind of accolade in a small town. 'All the girls got a turn to be Miss Bulls. The photo was awful.' Neil is keen to dig it out and show me. Sally insists she has no idea where it is.

Before too long, the girlfriend was jettisoned, Neil and Sally were going out, and they were driving from Palmerston North to Bulls so Neil could meet her parents. As they drove over the Bulls Bridge across the Rangitīkei River, Neil turned to Sally and said, 'I remember this bridge — I saved a girl's life here once.'

'I was puffing my chest out, and doing this,' Neil says, making himself look big and strong. And then, Sally says, he looked at her again and added: 'She looked a bit like you.' At which point Sally looked at him afresh and said, 'It *was* me!' And they unravelled the whole story.

The Rangitīkei Raft Race was held every summer; a big deal around those parts. Everyone from the surrounding towns came to play. There'd be family picnics all along the banks, and swimming in the river afterwards. Which is what 14-year-old Sally was doing in 1971, swimming with the quite swift current while the last of the homemade rafts finished the course. It wasn't until she tried to get out that she realised her foot really hurt and, when she lifted it above the water, she could see that a decent-sized piece of number 8 wire — probably from some kind of snare on the riverbed — had gone into her foot, hit the bone, and come out again at an angle.

'I thought, "Oh, gosh",' Sally says, wildly understating the drama of it, before spinning it the way a 14-year-old might. 'I thought, "It would be good if I got someone really good looking to rescue me." So I let myself drift down the river. I was looking at the shore to see who I could go "Help! Help!" to, and I saw these guys.'

Three of them, one of whom was Neil. She did her 'Help! Help!' routine, but unfortunately, with the foot underwater again and the wire out of sight, all Neil and his mates saw was a pretty girl waving at them. They cheerfully waved back. 'Then I was really a bit worried, because you get up to the rapids, and I thought, "Oh, man, I could drown here, for real." I couldn't swim, couldn't kick my feet, and a couple of times I went under, and then I panicked. That's when Neil came in, him and one of his mates.' They'd worked it out: not waving — drowning.

Neil insists she wasn't looking at him, she was looking at the other guy — Pete with the long blond hair — but Sally isn't having it. She remembers vividly what they all looked like — Neil with his Donna Summer vibe — even though her foot also really hurt and she was a bit preoccupied with that, despite simultaneously trying to make the most of the situation. Similarly, Neil says the whole rusty-wire-through-the-foot thing looked horrible, but it didn't stop him noticing her glorious red hair. The boys got her out of the river to safety, and sent her off to the emergency doctor, who injected a local anaesthetic and pulled the wire out. 'I was in trouble for being late home — my mother didn't believe me, because, once it was out, it didn't actually look like much.'

They spotted each other again a few weeks later. Peter Sinclair (yes, *the* Pete Sinclair from *C'Mon* and *Happen Inn* and later *University Challenge* fame) would host dances at the Lido in Palmerston North, and Neil and Sally saw each other — just a glance across the room, each of them ensconced with their own friends. Presence noted, and stored away.

Being in a spot of trouble with her parents was pretty much par for the course for Sally at this point. Her mum and dad owned the local dairy and were well respected in the community, but the general consensus was that Sally was hanging out with the wrong crowd, and there had been a couple of home visits from the local cop. Her parents were planning a move to Australia, and decided they'd send Sally on ahead to live with her brother. In the end, they couldn't sell the dairy and didn't make the move to join her. After 18 months of homesickness, Sally came back to Bulls.

Which is how she came to be driving across the bridge with Neil that day, and working out that the girl he'd saved was her. 'As soon as he said that, I just knew he looked really familiar. It had been a year-and-a-half, but yeah.'

'It was a big shock,' Neil says, 'because I had no idea whatsoever it was her. I think I was pretty stoned most of the time then. There was no way I thought Sally was the person — but now I think, how could I *not* see Sally was the person, with her hair colour? You were pretty distinctive.'

Remember that Sally had already decided Neil was The One, and he'd felt an intense attraction to her. The revelation now that he'd saved her life 18 months earlier cemented those feelings — wired them together, if you like. Fate, and Destiny, and a palpable sense of 'meant to be'.

They lived together for a year, which (as we've noted with other couples established in the 1970s) was shocking to all and sundry. Especially Sally's Catholic parents. 'Dad was ringing every week saying that my mother was so upset and she couldn't face people and I was living in sin, and that boy needs to marry you, blah blah blah. We were laughing about it, you know, and I said, "How ridiculous that we should get married at this age, that would just be stupid." Neil said, "Yeah, man, that'd be awful, we'd be *married*." And I said, "What? You mean it would be awful to be married to me?" And he said, "No, I didn't mean *that*." We had this huge fight, and then he said, "Okay, well, let's just get married!"'

Neil is delighted by this whole recollection. 'I did, too! It was halfway through the night.' Sally had somehow talked herself from 'Why on earth would we get married?!' to being engaged in one evening. The clincher was the realisation that a wedding would mean a toaster and an electric kettle and a number of other things they needed for their flat. There was a haircut for Neil, and a Catholic wedding, and the photos from 13 April 1974 show two beautiful kids — she was 17, he was 18 — dressed to the nines and misty-eyed.

Sally and Neil have three children — a daughter, Jasmine, born in 1976, and sons Joshua and Caleb, born in 1977 and 1980, respectively. We talk about the years they've spent living an unconventional life — a commune in Palmerston North called 'Wimbledon', and another in Motueka with a bunch of tobacco-leaf pickers. For some years they were members of a church that verged on being a religious cult, and now they have more questions than answers about God and religion. But the one constant has always been this sense that they are meant to be together, and they're still perfectly happy to cosy up in their house-bus for months at a time.

It's a terrific story, and I adored meeting Sally and Neil, but something felt slightly off during my visit. I could hear it on the tape when I listened back later — not the usual layered storytelling where one person makes an offer of a detail and the other picks it up and adds more. Sometimes, one of them would begin to say something and the other would shut it down, or head off in another direction. It made sense when Sally got in touch afterwards to tell me that, just before I'd arrived, she and Neil had 'had words', and were pretty mad with each other. I figured this explained the lack of eye contact between them, the reluctance to play the 'Yes, that's right! And also, *this* ...' game that couples usually engage in when they tell me their story, affirming each other and adding moments of magic to it.

It's one of the things Professor Donna Rose Addis talked about when we met — 'mood congruence' in retrieving memories. That when you're in your happy place, you will retrieve the positive episodic memories from all over your brain-office and put them together to tell a happy story. But on a shit day, you won't be in the right mood to grab all the sparkly bits. Which suddenly, while talking to Donna Rose, made me horribly anxious: by asking Sally and Neil to tell me their story when they were cross with each other, had I permanently damaged their memory of it? Ruined the story for them? Professor Addis, award-winning neuroscientist, promised me that I hadn't. What

Neil and Sally were retrieving that day was the *semanticised* version of their story — the one they had told often, with all the facts in place. 'If it's one that they've told many times before, there's going to be a core to it that can't be changed. In their case, it sounds more like a case of *how* they tell, and how they *engage* with it, and do they get *into* it.' On another day, in a different mood, they would still be able to whip around their brain-offices and put together more detailed, shared episodic memories. I hadn't broken anything. It would all still be there.

It was an interesting discovery for me. Remember that my theory right from the start was that a couple's shared story helps bind them together, because (a) it gives them a belief that they are meant to be with each other, and (b) the retelling of it re-creates those original emotions, and reignites their passion. We didn't achieve (b) with Neil and Sally that particular day, but (a) was still firmly in place. You can hear it in what each of them said when I asked about the significance of their river-rescue story.

> Sally: It definitely holds us together, yes. Because even though I'm an atheist now, I still think things are connected like that, so it's always been a strong feeling of mine. I've always had this feeling that it's Fate, or Destiny or something. I don't really believe in that sort of stuff, but I do where we're concerned.

Neil: Yeah, there are too many things that happened, and have happened since then that are almost … out of our control. It's like something's happened to keep us together, and you can call it 'him' or 'her' or whatever you want to, I suppose. We knew that something had brought us together.

I met up with Sally and Neil months later when they came to a show I was doing in Hamilton. They looked relaxed and happy, and — if possible — even younger and more vibrant than when I had met them on that bleak sort of day. Still certain that the way they met was all the proof they needed that they belong to each other. Which is impossible to argue with after 40-odd years.

CHAPTER 18

Not Always Plain Sailing

WE'VE MET LOTS OF PEOPLE who fell in love in an instant, and a few people who hated each other on sight. We've heard about relationships that had catastrophic starts, or took forever to get off the ground. In most of these tales, the drama happens either at the beginning or right at the end. But what if the drama happens in the middle: you fall in love, then out of love, then back in love? Or there's a connection, then a disconnection before you find each other again. Maybe one of you is already married, or things were going too fast, or there's an early deal-breaker — like maybe he spells it 'deel-braker' and you just can't take that sort of nonsense.

*

It was August 1973 when **Sandy** first set eyes on **Peter**. There was no bolt of lightning — not indoors, anyway, although it was a stormy night outside. Sandy had gone to dinner at her friend Patricia's place, along with half-a-dozen old school friends; a bunch of young women home from university for the holidays.

Pat had rustled up the troops for a particular reason. The night before, Pat had met a chap called Sean in a bar. Sean was taking leave from his ship and, in the course of striking up a conversation with Pat, had lamented the lack of friendly New Zealand girls about the place. If it was a pick-up line (it was a pick-up line), it worked a treat. Anxious to save our reputation as an open and friendly country (and possibly because people who live on small islands are hardwired to seek to expand the gene pool), Pat had invited Sean over to dinner at her house the next evening so he could meet her friends.

That afternoon, Sean rang Pat and asked if it would be okay to bring three other shipmates with him. Pat was sure she could stretch the food, so here they all were — Pat's posse of gals, and Sean's motley crew. 'My first thought,' Sandy says, 'was that they were definitely not my type. One looked vaguely interesting and even quite good-looking, but I could see that he would soon be claimed by my more attractive friends.' She was, however, charmed by their soft British accents and tales of life on the ocean waves as they all sat around the fire after dinner.

'Some initial pairings took place, and soon there was just Peter and three "left-over" girls sitting by the fire. I remember just listening as I continued to be lulled by his accent, exotic tales of the places he had been around the world, and the Isle of Wight where he had lived before he set sail as a 17-year-old deck officer in the British merchant navy. He didn't seem to stop talking! I noticed his curly black hair and very blue eyes.'

Some connections were made that night, but they didn't involve Sandy or Peter. That was that, then. Yet, inexplicably, in the days following, something made her want to contact Peter. He hadn't shown any special interest in her, and she didn't feel particularly attracted to him (apart from the blue eyes), but there was something about him and his boyish charm. 'He was quite different from all the boys I had known before. He didn't smoke dope, drink alcohol to excess, it seemed, or have long hair ... It became an overwhelming feeling. I *had* to make contact. I got books out of the library on the Isle of Wight. I thought about going there ... It all became a bit of a romantic dream that didn't have any basis and I didn't really understand it.'

Sandy decided to try to make contact by writing a letter, 'though I could only guess at his surname, and where do you address a letter to a man on a ship?' It was worth a shot, though, so she sent a letter with an incorrectly spelt name and a return address. 'Some weeks later, when I had all but forgotten, a letter came back to me.'

Remarkable, really, and if this was a simple kind of love story, that would be all we'd need. Letters exchanged increasing in romantic intensity, cue the wedding march, roll credits. Except for two things. By now, Sandy says she was over her 'brief romantic flight of the imagination' and she wasn't all that bothered about him anymore. And crucially this: 'His spelling was awful! Handwriting squiggly!' Spelling and handwriting really mattered to Sandy, an Education/ English double major. Totally understandable. You can't relish a *billet-doux* if it makes you want to take out your red pencil, make corrections in the margins and write back 'Must pay more attention in class.'

So that was it for Sandy. Other boyfriends came and went. Out of politeness, possibly, she continued to correspond with Peter, each time trying to ignore the atrocious spelling and ghastly handwriting. Eventually, a letter arrived saying his ship was arriving in Auckland and could they meet? 'I failed to make a date, decided not to bother and the letters stopped.' Life moved on. Apparently.

'But one night I did something I would never have contemplated before. I went to a concert alone in the Auckland Town Hall. I never went to anything by myself, and I would never have chosen this particular concert. It was the British folk group Fairport Convention, and I remembered Peter had spoken of them that night by the fire. As I walked into the Town Hall, the first person I saw was Peter. I could hardly believe it. I felt embarrassed and decided to pretend I hadn't seen him. I didn't think he'd seen me, but after I had sat for a few minutes there was a tap on my shoulder. The rest is history.'

Peter made several trips back to New Zealand on his ship, and Sandy travelled to the UK two years later. She finally got to see the Isle of Wight — the island she'd read about in those books at her local library in the first weeks after they'd met at Pat's dinner. On 29 August 1975, they were married on the Isle of Wight in the town of Ryde.

'Despite those initial wonderings and misconnections, our marriage has got better and better, and we are the greatest of friends. Our meeting was all about chance, and being in a certain place at a certain time. For me it was about following a feeling that didn't go away, and I have come to believe it was meant to be.'

Sandy and Peter Garman settled back here in Warkworth, in a little cottage by the sea. After the merchant navy, Peter spent most of his working life as a builder, and is now heavily involved in the coastguard. Sandy is a teacher. She says he has 'reinvented us as PPPPers — people pursuing personal projects'.

How do a seadog and a spelling-hound rub along together? 'We have very different interests. He is still a man of the sea, which I can only admire from a distance. I love books and literature and gardening. We have grown together and supported and enjoyed each other's interests, which has helped us do things we thought we could never do. I have crossed the Atlantic twice on the *Queen Mary* 2. Peter has greatly improved his spelling, and I have learned to decipher the handwriting. Well ... we have computers now.'

*

Michelle met **Brent** in 1987 at her friend's sister's engagement party in Foxton. She describes herself back then as 'an anxious, anorexic 21-year-old', and Brent as a 'hairy, pleasant, hardworking man of 27'. She says she knew the moment she saw him — in the afternoon at her friend's house before the party had even started — that Brent was The One.

Michelle and another friend, Gina, were staying at a motel nearby. While they were getting ready for the night, she told Gina, 'I'm having the one with the beard.' At which point Gina rolled her eyes. 'And this will not just be a one-night stand,' Michelle insisted, while Gina smirked. It was a big call for someone who was essentially nervous and shy. But, true to her word, Michelle pursued Brent all night. She was aware that while she might have been after 'a full-time man', he was more interested in the one-night stand she wasn't up for. Keen to know all about him, she asked him where he lived — the music was loud, and she thought he said 'Whanganui' and thought, 'Oh, God, not a long-distance relationship.' He was, however, so very cute she thought she might let that slide.

'We seemed to get along, and after the party we went back to our motel to have a spa. It was cold by this stage — about 2.30am. After he and his mate left our motel, a huge hailstorm hit. The thunder crashed and lightning lit up the whole sky. Gina was annoyed with me because she thought it was me, taking her photo with a flash. The lightning hit the fire station alarm, right next to where Brent was staying, so they didn't get much sleep.'

The next day, before Brent left Foxton, Michelle asked him for his address and phone number. She was thrilled to see it said 'Wainui', not 'Whanganui'. Wainuiomata is heaps closer to Lower Hutt, where she lived.

She rang him on the Monday to see how he was. After a few more phone calls, they went on their real first date, to Timothy's restaurant in Lower Hutt. 'A really posh place! That made it all the more scary. I was too scared to say much, too scared to say "boo" really.' Turned out Brent was a roofer, she worked for a real estate agency. Things went pretty well for a couple of months, until Michelle found out they were pregnant. She'd been told previously that, because she was so underweight and not menstruating, it was unlikely she could conceive, so this was a shock. Neither of them was ready for a child, so they opted for a termination. 'Tragic and traumatic as it was, we got through it and carried on. Then, after a year of me being needy and clingy, he broke things off with me.'

Michelle said she was devastated. She knew — had known from the start — that he was The One. She tried to give him some space, and leave him in peace. That worked for about a week, and then she phoned him 'to see if we could give it another go ... And we did.'

They went on to have three children — two of them conceived with the help of fertility drugs. They've bought and sold houses, and worked together in a family roofing business. They were married on New Year's Day in 2001 — Michelle says she decided that, because they were going into business together, they should have the same family name.

There is a story about the wedding she likes to tell. 'I was talking with a friend, and she said the most important things in a wedding are the dress and the photos, to which I agreed. She thought we were already married, so she said, "Of course, you already know this." I said, "But I'm not married." We started to organise my wedding that day, without hubby knowing.'

Eventually, she simply asked Brent if he wanted to get married on 1 January (her grandparents' wedding day) or

1 February (his mum's birthday). His reply was just as simple: 'What day am I *not* working?' The first of January it was, then, just six weeks later. 'A beautiful, sunny day — having rained like buggery the night before.'

Michelle describes them now, 30 years after that night in Foxton with the party and the spa and bolts of lightning, as best friends. 'I still think he's awesome.' He is semi-retired, pottering about at home and doing maintenance on their rental properties, and she works as a teacher-aide at the same school that Brent, his dad, and their three kids all went to. 'I have now had a 20-year relationship with that school, from when our oldest started to the present day.' She and Gina are still great mates, too. And Gina is possibly less inclined now, when Michelle makes a plan, to roll her eyes.

*

Small diversion while I think of it: 20 years ago when I was working as a magazine feature writer, I interviewed a costume designer who was working for New Zealand Opera. Tracey Grant Lord told me all kinds of fascinating things about the way costumes need to be constructed for an opera singer — nothing around the neck, which becomes sensitive and swells during the performance; wigs and hats are custom-made because the ability to make a good sound has a lot to do with the resonant nature of the skull, so good opera singers tend to have really big heads. And I've always remembered her telling me that some female opera singers prefer to wear boned corsets, especially around the diaphragm, because it gives them something to push against. That idea of having 'something to push against' struck me then as a pretty sweet metaphor for life. A challenge, something that tries to hold you back, which you can focus on and shove up against.

We've seen that phenomenon happening in some of the stories here: Tim and Jane in Chapter 8 being told on their wedding day that their marriage wouldn't last; Gavin and Tine, Jim and Soraya in the same chapter, and even Belynda and Martin in Chapter 6, all dealing with family crises that move things along. And in this next story, Jodie and Tony being nudged closer three times by an attack from an outside force.

*

Jodie and **Tony** first met in 1991 when they were both doing their nursing training — she was in her second year, he was in his third. Jodie was 37 years old and married; Tony was 21. 'On his twenty-first birthday he sat next to me in class and told me how his girlfriend, the love of his life, had just broken up with him. He was planning his twenty-first birthday party and his ex was invited, and he was worried how he was going to get through it. I thought he was a nice person and going through a rough time. He also had a cute bottom and an interesting collection of colourful braces and waistcoats.'

They were working through a psychiatric unit in their course: one week in class, followed by a three-week placement that could be anywhere in Canterbury. Without Jodie knowing anything about it, Tony twice swapped his rosters so he could work with her. 'I had no idea this was happening, but eventually we got to work together.'

On one shift they were looking after a patient who was a paranoid schizophrenic. 'He was in what was called "boundaries", which meant he could not leave his room, but the door was open and he could come and stand in the doorway and watch people passing. We were on the way to our meal beak and passed the room, and he started to come out into the corridor. Tony told him he had to go back into the room as he was on boundaries. The guy turned and went to walk into his room, then suddenly turned back and grabbed Tony and they fell to the ground. I called for help; the guy bit, spat, punched and kicked at Tony and, because he was in the throes of a psychotic episode, he was running on adrenaline and supercharged. It took 45 minutes for the staff to sedate him adequately to get Tony away from him.'

Their tutor asked Jodie to look after Tony and drive him home, then to pick him up again the following day and bring him back to the hospital. The tutor was sure if Tony had been left to come back to the hospital the following day on his own, he would not have come. The tutor was right: Tony was not going to come back, and considered giving up nursing.

'I picked him up every day for the next week and took him to the hospital. He finished his third year, sat his final exams and I didn't see him again for quite some time.'

It was a deeply traumatic event, but you can still see that, underneath the surface, something else was happening between them. We have Tony getting rosters rearranged so he could spend time with Jodie; and Jodie caring enough about Tony to take responsibility for ensuring he kept coming to work. A pull towards each other, of wanting to be in each other's orbit, and of mutual concern.

They met again the following year. Jodie was in town with a friend, heading for the movies. 'We were going to *Silence of the Lambs*. I spotted Tony and asked him to join us. Interesting connection — we have a psych theme developing. But that was all there was to it; I was still married.'

Not just a psych theme — something of an attack theme. 'Next time, I met Tony in town. He was flatting with his sister, and they had had a huge row and she had thrown most of their crockery at him.' Jodie suggested that since she had a spare room and was now separated, he could stay with her until he found another flat.

That was in 1992, and Tony still hasn't found another flat. They were married in 1998 when Jodie was 44 and he was 28. 'Initially, there were gasps of horror in the family when they found out there was a 16-year age gap. But eventually everyone got used to the idea. We were even a hot topic of gossip at polytech for a short time, until something more interesting captured their attention.'

They are now grandparents, which Tony enjoys telling people. 'You can see them doing the maths. Usually he gets comments about starting early, or ageing well. Generally people aren't bothered about the age gap now: grey hair does a lot to even out the years.'

*

If we describe relationships in terms of their shape, these three are like donuts — an initial meeting that undeniably sparks something, then a hole in the middle before they properly join together. The holes here were small: a few months for Sandy and Peter, and Jodie and Tony; and just a week of no contact for Michelle and Brent (although they had a year of struggling with sadness before that complete break). I like these stories because they're hopeful, and remind us that it doesn't all have to go smoothly from the beginning to turn out great in the end. There can be hiccups and breakups and doubts, and you can survive them. That donut-hole in the middle might even last 13 years. Let's go meet Elizabeth and Tom.

CHAPTER 19

Sometimes It's Really Complicated

SOME STORIES ARE EASY TO TELL, not just because they romp along from one moment to the next, but because they involve only the two people at the centre. But if there is an affair, or a first family before the second one is created, then other people — and a whole range of other emotions — are involved. Which is why some stories are kept secret.

Tom and Elizabeth's story, though, deserves to be told. It is beautiful, and remarkable, and rare. I don't have favourites, but, if I did, this might be it. For reasons that will become clear, I'm going to tell it in a way that doesn't identify the players — where they live, their real names, what they look like, specific dates. All you need to know is that Elizabeth is warm and bright and softly spoken; and Tom is older, a retired farmer, and a man of few words. She is the talker; he says 'Mm-hmm' a lot and nods at her; they laugh at all the same things; and their laughter sounds good together.

Before and after I meet with them, we talk about why they wanted to offer their story for this book. Elizabeth explained it this way. 'I was once at the hairdressers and Sarah, this gorgeous young thing, loved (like I do) "people stories". She told me the story of her great-grandmother who got pregnant at 16. She was in service in Scotland. The story was about how this brave lady worked her way into a position where she could raise this child. An amazing story, and we talked about how Sarah must keep this story alive in her family, because it is precious and courageous, but has rarely been talked about. So … back to present-day me and my small family. Sometimes I have seen my daughter struggle to explain how her family came about, and sometimes I think that is because she feels the hurt that we have left in our wake, or feels the hurt herself. And it isn't all that fair to her. It's time that we held our heads up and told our story for what it is. I would like to think that those who have chosen to be our friends can hear our story, that our shared grandchildren can hear the story of love and laughter, and not hear some whispered tale of misery and hurt.'

So let's give that a go …

In the 1980s, Elizabeth left the small North Island town she'd grown up in and moved south, picking up casual jobs on various farms. She liked sheep farms best — plenty of animals to care for, and working dogs for company. She was offered work on Tom's farm, and arrived at Labour Weekend during tailing season, a pretty stressful time on a sheep farmer's calendar. It's a tricky business, getting those rings on skittish lambs' tails, and the dogs can go a bit crazy with lambs bouncing around and breaking off and needing to be brought back into line. 'If you can get on with somebody when you've just met them and you're going tailing, you're going to do well,' Elizabeth says. 'He didn't yell at me once — no shouting, no foul language.' The tailing done, she was offered a permanent place on the farm and stayed for several years.

Tom was married with children. They were conservative, rural people. Nevertheless, Tom and Elizabeth fell in love and, at some point, began an affair. When she became pregnant, there were few options. She wanted this child, and she loved the baby's father, but a farmer can't leave his farm. Tom's wife had worked things out by then — the affair, and the baby — but, as deeply traditional people, they didn't divorce. 'I always hoped we could be together, but it wasn't to be,' Elizabeth says. 'We decided I needed to leave, so I went home, where everybody goes, home to their mum and their dad.'

When Amber was born, Elizabeth threw herself into being a single parent with total focus. She had strong family support, huge love for this child, and she found a new career which she loved. There was occasional contact from Tom in the shape of birthday cards for Amber in the first few years, but they stopped arriving in the mid-1990s.

Meanwhile, down south, Tom and his first wife's marriage deteriorated. They sold the big farm when the kids grew up, bought a smaller one, and then moved into town. He hoped each shift would make things better between them, but it never did. Eventually, Tom's wife left him.

By then, Tom had had no contact at all with Amber and Elizabeth for seven years. Living alone now, some friends and one of his grown-up children encouraged him to look for them. Neither Tom nor Elizabeth are sure how relevant this is, but I find it fascinating that Tom's two children from his first marriage were both adopted, and have looked for and found their birth mothers. So the idea of searching for missing family wasn't a new one for Tom's whānau, and may have informed part of his decision to find his.

As it happened, at exactly the time Tom decided to reach out, 13-year-old Amber told her mother she'd like to write a letter to her dad. I ask Elizabeth what Amber knew then about her father. 'She always knew as much as she wanted to know. She had a photo, and she had some birthday cards, but she wasn't overly curious. Then in the January of that year she said, "I'm going to write to my dad and tell him about me."'

Fourteen years after she left the farm — and entirely out of the blue — Elizabeth gets a phone call from Tom. She remembers the exact date easily. ('Some things get burned into one's memory.') 'He said he would like to see Amber. He expected me to hang up. I said, "I'll talk to you later," because Amber was running around and I thought we needed to talk privately first. He said, "Oh, well, ring me back." I said, "No, because your wife will answer." He said, "No, she's not with me anymore." So I rang back! Amber went to bed and we talked for three hours. It was a bleary-eyed day at work the next day!'

'For the next few *weeks*!' Tom adds, both of them laughing. 'We talked every night!' Three months, actually — long phone calls well into the evening, catching up and reconnecting, getting to know each other again. Elizabeth encouraged Amber to finish that letter to Tom, and he wrote back to his daughter, suggesting they could meet if she would like to. They set a date.

'But we knew Tom and I had to meet first, had to get that out of the way so the meeting could be all about Amber.' They planned their own reunion in Picton. 'I went to ask my boss if I could leave early to go on the Picton ferry to meet Tom. I said, "I better tell you why." He's a romantic, he was lovely about it.'

Elizabeth was a bundle of nerves on the trip across the Cook Strait — heart pounding all the way. When the ferry doors opened, she considered staying on board and going home. But there was Tom, waiting for her, steady and calm. I ask him if he was just doing a good impression of someone who wasn't nervous, but he smiles and says simply, 'No.' He had left home at 6am, driven up, booked a motel, bought food, arranged everything.

It went at least as smoothly as that first Labour Weekend tailing. 'It was like we'd never been apart, because we had been talking every night for three months. Even if it's not face-to-face, you re-establish a huge amount of connection. Then it's just the physical connection,' Elizabeth says. 'That was just wonderful. We had a lovely weekend, didn't we? Didn't want to part. But Tom went back south and me back north. It was a bit sad, wasn't it? It was just totally "this is how it should be", it was wonderful. What a lot of years we've — Well, we shouldn't say "wasted", but we've got time to make up for.'

As Elizabeth says all this (she is 'the talker' after all), Tom smiles and nods and does his affirmative 'Mm-hmm' with something like Buddhist serenity. He mentions his long trip home, hours of driving through winter fog, alone. Two weeks later, he comes north again — by plane this time — to meet his daughter for the very first time. It is the day before Amber's fourteenth birthday.

'I had one instruction for him from Amber,' Elizabeth says, smiling. '"Please don't hug me." But he did, he couldn't help himself. He is a bit of a huggy person. For Tom — I might be speaking for you here — but it was a bit like meeting the baby for the first time.' There is a firm 'Mm-hmm' from Tom. 'I've read about meetings with biological parents and children, how that rush of emotion is quite like that first rush when baby is born.'

And as she says this, it occurs to me that the way she had just described her reunion with Tom two weeks before had the same quality: they had fallen in love again that weekend in Picton. To my ears — practised now at hearing people describe the moment their souls collided — it contained the identical rush of emotion you hear when people talk about falling in love at first sight, even though this was almost two decades after they'd initially laid eyes on each other. They had chosen not to tell me any details about their other beginning back on the farm before Amber was conceived, but this second beginning sounds exactly like all our other stories of two people falling in love.

Back to Tom and Amber. I ask Tom what it was like, then, meeting his daughter for the very first time. 'It was okay, yeah, good,' he says, and grinds to a halt. 'That's as much as you'll get,' Elizabeth says sweetly. She is used to people keeping their emotional cards close to their chest — Amber is wired the same way. That day at the airport, they'd managed to lose their car keys, which gave Amber a job to do, a handy distraction — rushing about, looking for them, asking strangers if they'd seen keys anywhere. 'She keeps her emotions back here. She was polite, respectful, engaging, and pretty happy.'

Tom continued to visit Amber and Elizabeth; Elizabeth travelled south to visit Tom. They took care to move their own relationship along slowly, letting Amber set the pace for coming together as family. It went surprisingly smoothly, and eventually they bought a house in the North Island and all lived for the first time under one roof. They describe Tom's parenting style then as being a bit like a grandparent, indulging Amber, letting her bat her eyelids to get what she wanted. But most of all, Tom says, it was about always giving her their time.

There were revelations. Tom's siblings and nieces were blown away about how much Amber looked like their family, and especially like Tom's older sister. Amber had never looked much like her mother's family (Elizabeth had sometimes joked she must have been swapped in the hospital), so meeting her aunts and uncles and cousins, and seeing family photos filled with people who looked like her, gave her a sense of belonging, like putting pieces of a puzzle together.

The three of them hadn't been together all that long when Amber asked her mother if she would mind very much if she changed her family name to her dad's. The question was asked nervously, because Amber thought her mother would be upset. She wasn't. 'We gave her the "change of name" papers for her birthday.' It was also the catalyst for Tom and Elizabeth's marriage — a way for everyone to share the same name, just like other families who start out in a more conventional way.

They kept the wedding low-key. Tom's other children didn't want to be there — there may have been initial support for finding Amber but that had since faded, and they still refuse to meet either her or her mother. But Elizabeth's family were there, and some of Tom's other relatives and several old friends. The best part of their wedding day was when a teenage Amber made a speech saying that having her mother and father married to each other was what she had been dreaming of her whole life.

A decade on, Amber is married and has a daughter of her own. Elizabeth and Tom live nearby, and are doting grandparents. In the photographs of them all, you can't see any missing years. Elizabeth says that when they first reconnected, she asked Tom endless questions about that time in between — what he'd done, what he'd thought, what he'd felt. There had been difficult times for them both, so much heartbreak, and she needed to address it. They're alike in many ways, but they were different in this: Tom was already eager to move forward. Eventually, she says, she ran out of questions, and that's when the relationship they have now blossomed. Soulmates, they both say, without regrets, and with plenty of time stretching ahead of them. They have already been together more years than they were apart.

I tell them about my theory — that a great story binds couples together — and theirs is undeniably a great story with possibly *the* greatest happy ending. Elizabeth thinks about this for a while, and then — in part — disagrees. It is not their first story that binds them — the time on the farm, the first falling in love. 'That didn't bring us together. I think that was about such stolen moments, really. And difficult, and guilty.'

It is the *second* story — of the phone call out of the blue, and the months of talking, and finally meeting — that they treasure. 'To just then come together and have the pure joy!' That meeting in Picton is the date they celebrate each year. Not their wedding anniversary, but that day when Elizabeth found the courage to get off the boat, and Tom made sure everything was ready.

CHAPTER 20

Storytelling as Therapy

AS I FINISH WRITING each chapter, I fire it off to the people involved so that they can fact-check it and add or subtract details. The return emails are always warm and enthusiastic, and often they tell me they've sat down to read it together and that this was a hugely pleasurable thing, which is a lovely image in my head — couples dotted about the country on long winter nights or summer evenings, reading their shared story by an open fire or on the deck with a cocktail. I like to imagine them taking turns with reading it out loud, or passing the pages between them, and saying stuff like 'What are you laughing at?' or 'Hurry up, I've finished this one.'

Occasionally, people ask for (and are given) pseudonyms; and once, when I'd given them pseudonyms, they ask to have their real names put back because they like the way it sounds, and it is, after all, 'a true story'. No one pulls out or changes their mind about having their story published — just the odd clarification or occasional obfuscation. This thing is making people happy.

By now, I'm feeling pretty convinced of my initial theory: that these stories of how couples meet — the romantic, absurd, serendipitous, convoluted, scandalous, breathtaking moments of connection — help to weave pairs of lives together. As we have seen, they do this in two ways: as 'proof' to them that they were meant to begin this couple-journey; and also because, as they retell them, they go back to those first falling-in-love feelings and rekindle their passion. Seriously, get a room.

But then it occurs to me that this is a less-than-scientific study (Wait! What?! Not science-y?!), because all of these couples are self-selecting. Of *course* they're going to agree with my theory, because anyone who thinks 'We might have a great story but it doesn't matter to us and serves no purpose' isn't going to bother to get in touch. These couples believe the story matters so much that they've offered it up for a book. It's a thing they tell at dinner parties and to their kids, and they are secure enough in their relationship to throw themselves under the spotlight on these pages. Therefore and ergo, here's a question: Is it possible that it is The Great Relationship that makes the story of their meeting sound great? Rather than The Great Story that makes the great relationship?

In which case, wouldn't it be useful and a bit more science-y to work out whether a couple *in trouble* might fix that trouble by recalling a great story about them both? Some kind of control experiment, I believe they call it.

I needed, therefore, to talk to someone who is in the business of talking with couples who are in trouble. Which is why I spent a happy afternoon with leading psychologist and relentlessly positive human Sara Chatwin. Talking to couples in crisis is not the only thing she does — Sara has spent a couple of decades helping sportspeople, businesses, families and individuals with stress, motivation and life skills, and she pops up regularly on radio and TV to say wise and helpful things. Some couples come to her because they need to get a bit of zing back after 20 years, or want help adjusting to being parents as well as partners. Sara and I have met here and there; she's as fit and energetic as you'd expect someone who advises athletes to be, and as bright and clear as you'd want someone who counsels the lost and confused to be. Spend an hour with Sara with her rapid-fire delivery and general effervescence, and the world is better almost instantly.

As I walk up the path to her house, I am deeply aware that understanding relationships is what she does for a job, and I am just an enthusiastic amateur. It's like I'm going around to the local garage with my car and saying to the mechanic, 'There's a noise in the front of it like a mongoose with hiccups — I reckon it's the diff'.' I should probably keep my theories to myself.

But of course I don't. I blurt out my 'great How We Met stories bind people together' hoo-ha before the kettle has even boiled.

'Oh, I like that! I haven't actually heard that before, so this is very new and unique. I think you've probably hit it.' (This is, just quietly, a really good start.) 'I think that a shared story in which both partners are the important parts — the "actors" or the "main characters" — is a nice one.' In fact, Sara goes further and says she thinks you possibly *have* to have something like a terrific shared story as the years go by. 'Because in the first couple of years, you've still got that hormonal heady rush and they can't really do a lot wrong. Then after that, statistics will bear out that around year three you're going, "Oh, okay, now I've seen him or her in *that* light doing *that*, looking like *that* in the morning and being like *that* on the weekend" and the glow is a little tarnished. I think if you have that memory, and if you have that story which you can go back to and draw upon, it probably would galvanise people together. I like your theory, because I've *seen* it.'

She likes it, too, that I've mostly chosen couples who have been together 15 years or more, when the relationship is bedded in. She sees a difference in the quality of a relationship depending on how long couples have been together. In those first years — say two to five — they are still very attracted to each other, and it's still very sexy and all the rest of it, but they're not quite solid. 'The relationship that they're in doesn't give them full confidence or security, surety, certainty, because they're still looking around. I reckon it's when you get to that point when you're *not* looking around, when that person still does it a bit for you sexually, and still does it a lot for you in terms of friendship and trust and being your confidante, that you've got it. It's about maintaining that.'

The national average, she says, is seven years before you get a divorce — the old 'cycle of seven' we talked about back in Chapter 4. When she sees couples who have been together for 20 years, the first thing she tells them is to give themselves a medal: they've already achieved three times the national average. 'It's about remembering the good stuff and talking about it. If you talk about the good stuff on a regular basis, your relationship's good. If you focus on the negative stuff and talk about that on a regular basis, there ain't nothing good going to come of that.' Which echoes Professor Addis in Chapter 10: the difference between *savouring* the details of the good memory rather than *ruminating* over the negative generalities. 'It's about having that positive conversation about your relationship.'

'In terms of this book's journey, you're going to be helping people's marriages,' she declares with huge enthusiasm, before pretending to be irritated. 'You're going to be doing my job. I'm not liking that at all!'

Of course, Sara points out, there's more to a relationship than how two people meet. 'When people come together — a man and a woman, or a woman and a woman, a man and a man — they bring different genetic stuff with them, different nurture, and environmental stuff. But generally, if you have two people who come together from very similar family backgrounds and they've had similar educations and similar this and that, it should all match up.'

People get into trouble, she says, when they lose sight of the things they first loved about each other because of things outside their relationship: work stress, raising kids, illness, financial pressure, other relationship responsibilities — the things that Jeremy and I call 'poo through the windows'. 'But you can close the windows,' Sara says, 'and you're just safe.'

While Sara hasn't (so far) asked couples in strife to specifically focus on a shared story of 'how they met' as therapy, what she *does* do is deliberately take them back to the beginning of their relationship. First, she will meet with them individually to get their unique story; this is important, because when people come together with different genetics and from different environments, they will have different perspectives on things and she needs to hear both. Then she will bring them together for a couples session. 'Initially, it can start off a bit nasty and a bit "She does this", "He did that", "It's his fault", "That's why it happened"; the blaming, the guilting, all of that.'

She leads them away from the conflicted stuff and tries to tap into the story of what brought them together. 'By the end of the session, I'm talking about the things that made them love each other or the things that drew them together. That's part of the story that you're talking about,' she says. And it is effective, this guided approach to retrieving episodic memory, with Sara working like an external hippocampus to help them find detailed memories in those boxes in their brain-office. 'They often walk away going "Ah, I forgot that! Yeah, I remember that now. Wow, that was a really cool feeling. If we can get some of that back ..." The comment that I make is, well, you had it, so you can get it back. You've just got to do a bit of work to uncover it.'

I tell her that recovering those first falling-in-love memories with couples for this book has led to the 'I'll just let you two get a room' scenario. 'I often have the same situation,' she says. 'By the end of the session they're walking out of my door feeling better, not worse. That's really important to me as a therapist.'

So those original emotions really can be reignited, just by talking about it? 'Absolutely. You're tapping into them again.

Those emotions may have been covered over by time, by children, by experiences ... People get together, their finances fall apart, they're bankrupt, they might have a child who's terribly sick ... The love and passion and the initial feelings that brought people together just go by the wayside and they're covered by all these, what I call, "life layers". Just layers of life. When people come to therapy with me, it's about stripping that stuff off and allowing the good stuff to shine through again.'

Which makes it sound really simple, except that after you've asked what they originally liked about each other — and you get all that fizzy, heady, horny, romantic stuff — you've got to then talk about how that person might have changed from being your dream lover to your nightmare cohabitant. 'He's mean now' or 'She says nasty things' or whatever it is that has led to the wheels falling off your relationship-wagon. Navigating them through that takes proper psychology skills.

And then Sara adds something I find really fascinating: 'For some people who have, in their own words, disastrous relationships, they might go: "Actually we got together for a night, had a baby and we tried." Maybe that's just not enough. That fits in with your theory, because they haven't had time to create a *story*. I'm not a huge proponent of one-night stands on that basis, because I just don't think you have all the nice, fuzzy stuff to build on.'

I'm glad she's brought up the one-night stand. It's a phenomenon I've been tossing around in my head while reading all these stories of how people meet. What if the relationship hadn't survived — would they still be tales we'd want to tell and hear? What would a book full of wild one-night stands be like? Sara reckons people might find that amusing for a bit, but eventually it would just be sad. 'There's no romance, no nice bits. It's a caveman, physical thing that anybody can really do if they're a bit bored. There's just no story there.'

Not that there's anything wrong with meaningless sex on occasion — a girl's gotta eat, right? Boys, too. But Sara reaches for a delightful metaphor: a one-night stand isn't a sandwich, it's just two bits of bread being banged ('scuse the pun) together. A meal, but not a sustaining one. I like the way she thinks.

I can imagine that a one-night stand could well have the frisson, bodies colliding, risk taking, and an element of happy coincidence that these two people ended up in the same place at the same time and were available to each other. But if they never saw each other again? Meh. Would we care that you spent a night on a yacht, or shagged in a shower block by the Margaret River? Probably not. Those stories from Warren and Faye and Maeve and Declan are magical because they were a *beginning.*

Which means — ta-da! — the great relationship must be responsible for imbuing at least some of the magic, retrospectively, into the great 'How We Met' story. The magic, Dear Reader, is passed backwards as well as forwards. This is a two-way street. Just let that settle in your mind for a bit; we will talk about it some more soon.

At the same time as helping to answer that question, Sara is also seriously confirming here that one of the tools for knocking a wonky relationship back into shape is the shared narrative. She is clear that if you're thrown into a relationship before you have time to make a story together, as a therapist she would find herself short of a pretty important tool.

Are relationships always hard work? 'It shouldn't be hard work all the time — you've got to work at relationships, but not the whole time.' Sara says that if it feels like Groundhog Day and you're waking up every morning to 'walk backwards through mud', it's possible you're not with the right person. 'But my key point here is that often the relationship is not crap, it's other stuff. Look at that other stuff. Don't just write your relationship off.'

It would be crazy to spend an afternoon with a relationship expert and not ask for some hot tips to take home for your single mates, right? Here's one: Don't be too specific about your love map. Sara says our definitions of beauty, of the kind of person we find attractive, or the age we're looking for in a partner, are all too narrow. She, for example, has never liked tattoos; it used to be part of her definition of the kind of person she could not be attracted to. 'And now I've got this amazing person who's got a few tattoos here and there. My definition broadened because he made me feel the way I wanted to feel in a relationship. It's about feeling special. I'd never dated anybody with tattoos. Now, I couldn't care less about them. In fact, I like them. Not that I'm rocking out to get any myself ...'

She tells her single girlfriends that there is no such thing as a man-drought — it's just that their definition of what they'll date is quite narrow. 'Take the blinkers off, flop it out there, leave it all out there and just walk through your life seeing who makes you feel good.'

That thing of wanting to be recognised by someone else as 'special' is important to us, Sara says — here we are, standing at a bar on a planet that features 7 billion other people and we want someone to notice us. Sara reckons this probably explains one of the mysteries thrown up by couples like Declan and Maeve, who argued (albeit cheerfully) about who chased whom.

'People like to think they stood out of the crowd for someone. Some of that's down to pride ... I would like to think that I didn't chase the boys; I think a lot of girls don't want to be the chaser, even if we are. It goes back to that primal "caveman dragging the cavewoman by the hair into the cave" kind of deal. You will find some girls who chase boys and, in gay couplings, it's not a gender-related issue at all — although perceptions might still be different about who did the chasing.' She says she has seen it start a few fights, but at some point it becomes neutral. 'You get together, it doesn't really matter who chased who.'

What *does* matter is having a little bit of magic somewhere and reliving it from time to time. And the magic doesn't have to be about how you met. In a therapy session with someone like Sara, you might be able to recover a great story about yourselves that you had forgotten, and use that. Or you might find magic on Tinder.

'I have a really neat friend who met someone on Tinder. This is fairly recent — they've been together for three years now. The Tinder thing was a little bit magic. Sure, there were all of these ungodly couplings at first, and this person went on dates and went, "Oh, my God, this is just crazy! This Tindering thing? *What*ever!" Then they met this really nice person and they went: "No, I don't believe she's *that* nice." Then they went out with her and they did a few really cool things. But it was the Tinder thing that sparked it, and the flame ignited and they created something really special. It was that online, sort of forced getting together — "Swipe! There we go! There's one! No, I don't want *them*!" But then they got to get a little bit of magic. So you don't necessarily have to *meet* and it's magic, but, if you persevere a bit, somewhere down the track there will be those little magical things that you can draw on.'

Which is entirely true. Let's go meet Kym and Dave, a couple of gay funeral directors who hooked up on the internet for a one-night stand; and a Kiwi in London who met a woman from Poland online and brought her home to Invercargill.

CHAPTER 21

Clicking and Swiping

TINDER, ESTABLISHED 2012, HAS a user base of around 50 million people, and was valued in 2017 at US$3 billion. It comes in at number one on the top-grossing app charts, beating Candy Crush, Netflix and Pandora. My relationship is pre-Tinder, but I have enjoyed the odd evening with friends, helping them swipe left (eew) or right (ooh), and one friend in particular entertains me at random intervals by texting screenshots of the more idiosyncratic profile pictures that turn up on her phone. Anything that involves really bad Photoshop (his face is a *completely* different colour from those washboard abs) or the unexpected placement of a horse (how did he get it *there*?) gets a big thumbs-up from me.

We can take the piss out of Tinder (and we can also have serious discussions about whether, in some scenarios, it becomes a tool for objectification rather than empowerment), but there is no argument about the powerful role it currently plays in how people meet. It used to be at university, through friends, in a bar, at the office ... Crikey, why am I telling you — you've just been reading about it. We are already having to explain all this historical nonsense to our kids, prefacing the talk with 'Back in the olden days, we used to meet in a room ...' And then clarify with 'No, not "chat"; a literal room.' The phone app is now so much the leading tool of engagement that some of us don't know there used to be another way. If there is a second edition of this book in 15 years' time, every chapter will begin 'So I swiped right ...'

To make it a proper history lesson, we should also explain that Tinder didn't invent the phenomenon of matching people up via technology. There were early devices called computers that were so big they sat on a table and, if you turned them on before breakfast, they'd be ready to work by morning tea. Quite a few people had them and, if you didn't, you could pop around to a mate's house and use theirs. True story.

It was by using one of these computer things in 2006 that **Kym Zelton** met **David Zelton** on the NZDating website. They weren't both called 'Zelton' back then. In fact, that night they weren't calling themselves 'Kym' and 'Dave' either. As is often the case in the gay community (where some people are closeted, and others — like many of us — simply prefer a level of privacy or the opportunity to adopt a persona), their profiles featured fake names. Thirty-four-year-old Dave was calling himself 'Brad' and was looking for a casual hook-up. Thirty-three-year-old Kym was 'Kane', and he was looking for Mr Right. 'Well, you found him,' Dave says.

I bloody adore Kym and Dave. They look like a couple of truck drivers and sound like kindy teachers. Kym has tattoos, and he's into cars and also disco. He's the talker. Dave's got a dry sense of humour and punctuates their chat with a well-placed 'That's right', and quick summaries of Kym's longer stories. Kym often calls Dave 'Mildred', and you can't quite tell if Dave loves this, but, if he didn't, he would have surely said something by now.

Through the dating site, Kym/Kane gets an email from Dave/Brad, and they arrange to meet at Kym's house on a Saturday night. Both of them remember being wildly nervous, but Dave says they 'clicked straight away'. They drank a lot of coffee, Dave stayed the night and left about 8am, saying he needed to be elsewhere. He came back at lunchtime and asked if he could come in for another coffee and a chat, and he has never left.

They are opposites, Kym says, and Dave slips in: 'Because he's the bad egg, and I'm the good egg.' Kym explains he went off the rails in his twenties, dealing with his sexuality and with depression, and dabbled in some things he shouldn't have.

Some dumb, stupid stuff. And then he came right, worked on himself, started doing the right things in the right way. He was ready to settle down and make a family. 'Lo and behold, this wonderful gift arrives on the doorstep. This is the way I look at it. I still think, "Why? How come I'm so lucky?" Dave and I know several others who have had a civil union or whatever and they've split up ... Well, for starters it doesn't help because they sleep around on one another, they have these stupid open relationships, so of course it puts a spanner in the works. But, yeah, I don't know what it is with us two that's made it work, why we've come so far. But it's a true blessing. We just get on with it every day.'

Dave hadn't gone off the rails in his youth in the same way Kym did, but he struggled with his sexuality in his teens; pretended he was straight to keep his family happy, got engaged to a girl at some point. But Kym's family embraced Dave immediately, especially his mother. Kym says back when he thought he was straight he'd bring girls home and his mother never liked them, but she has always adored Dave. 'She's been like a mum to me,' Dave says.

Kym's mother suffered a severe stroke a little while ago and now needs 24/7 care, so they visit her often in her rest home. The couple shares their house with Kym's stepdad, the man Kym thinks of as his father. They are also raising two boys —

Kym's cousin's kids, Josh and Byron — both now in their teens. Previously, the kids were living in state care, but Kym and Dave applied to be their caregivers and were accepted. The boys call them both 'Uncle Dad'. Josh has minor special needs, and for a long time he didn't talk, but he has found his voice now.

'There's still a long road ahead for him. There is the possibility that he may, as an adult, have to go into community housing to live. We will do as much as we can to prevent it, because that would be the last resort for us,' Kym says. 'We just want the best for Josh. If he was to become a trolley boy at Pak'nSave, I'd be as proud of him doing that as if he was a scientist.'

So they have a home and a family together. I ask them if they believe in soulmates and they say 'Yes, I do' one after the other, like they're saying vows, which sounds really sweet.

They said those vows for real on 30 August 2008 in a civil union ceremony, which is when Dave took Kym's last name. 'I wanted to be like Mum and Dad, and other people,' Kym says — one couple, one name. Dave felt the same way, although he says they find it hilarious now when they get mail addressed to 'Mr and Mrs Zelton' and have to phone them to say, excuse me, we're Mr and *Mr.* Occasionally, in business and social situations, people will say, 'Kym Zelton and Dave Zelton ... Are you two brothers?' To which Dave will say, 'No, he's my husband,' and he quite enjoys watching them think this through. 'We're a couple, we're husbands,' Kym states firmly. And Dave adds, 'We're one.'

They are one in business, too. When they first met, Kym was working as a baker and Dave was in sales and marketing, but now they're both funeral directors and Dave runs the Christchurch branch of a funeral home. They love personalising funerals — blasting Credence Clearwater in the hearse if that was the deceased's favourite band — and they're trialling the idea of evening funerals for people who might find that easier or more fitting than going to a service during the day.

Back when Kym was working in the bakery, he couldn't wear jewellery and didn't like being without his wedding ring. So he has a tattoo on his arm — the date of their civil union in roman numerals and, intriguingly, two women's symbols intertwined. I ask why those, and not the symbols for men. He says he has always found the ones with the pointy arrows a bit rude, and preferred the ones with the crosses. It is perfect reasoning, and looks good on a man who has made up his own rules — and played by them — for most of his life. With the date sitting there on Kym's forearm, there's no chance that either of them will ever forget their anniversary. Not that they would — it is a big deal for them, celebrated a couple of years ago with a cruise: the honeymoon they hadn't been able to manage because of other commitments in 2008.

Do they remember the date that Brad turned up at Kane's place for a hook-up? Kym tries to sound casual, but ends up being very specific. 'It was about January 18, 2006.' Dave confirms that this is indeed correct. Like so many other couples, they don't make a huge fuss of it, but they remember it every year — pop down to the pub for a couple of quiet ones to celebrate. Then back to the home Dave arrived at once for a coffee and a chat, and never left.

*

Terry Frisby is an old mate — he and my husband, Jeremy, used to be half of a comedy troupe (I like saying 'troupe' because it makes them sound like vaudevillians) called The Brat Pack, in the late 1990s and early 2000s. The other half of the troupe were Chris Brain and Rhys Darby and, together, they performed everywhere from Ashburton to the Edinburgh Fringe. Terry moved to London in 2000, and we'd occasionally swing by his flat while en route to gigs or festivals or holidays on that side of the world.

Ania Frisby is a new friend — Terry brought her with him when he came home to New Zealand in 2010. We'd regularly swing by their house in West Auckland for poolside barbecues before they moved south to Terry's hometown of Invercargill in 2016, and we swing by their new house now when we're in the neighbourhood, mostly for comedy gigs that Terry produces and MCs. He has a day job as a business manager, and Ania, originally from Poland, became a New Zealand police officer in 2017.

I had a vague notion that Terry and Ania had met on a blind date in London, but when I discovered that they'd hooked up through a dating website I asked them to use the same *modus operandi* to tell their stories by email, independently of each other. Because that's kind of how a dating website works, right? You present yourself blind, into an open forum: it's like giving a performance without a live audience. You have to tell your whole story before you find out how people react.

I received two separate emails — there had been no consultation, no collaboration between them. There are some delightful similarities: both reveal a level of reluctance to get amongst internet dating, and say they were pushed into it by friends (although Terry had a fall-back position for what to do with the experience if it went tits-up); both had rescue plans in place when they met in the real world (Terry's wingman almost derailed their first date); we see them get two shots at first impressions — online and in person (Terry gets points off for his profile pic, but points *on* for actually looking like it); and we learn that, even on the internet, personality can eat looks for breakfast. Plus — bonus for us — Terry reveals a secret he has kept from Ania all this time.

Ania first ...

> It was 2007; I lived in London at the time. A friend of mine, Alex, was really concerned about my 'single' status. I must have complained to him that I was getting bored or something, because he started telling me stories about his friend from work who signed up to this dating website 'mysinglefriend.com'. Alex said his friend kept meeting new guys every week; she was going out with them to all sorts of different events. He described it as being super fun and certainly not boring. He suggested he could help me sign up for the dating website. I was always very sceptical about internet dating. What's more, I have to admit, I thought internet dating was for losers ... But after three months of convincing, I finally let Alex create a profile for me on the website.
>
> My flatmate Sylwia and I, like typical girls, started looking through the catalogues of men on the dating web and, oh boy, did we make fun of them! I really wasn't serious about this website, and my scepticism was

still there. I said to Alex and Sylwia that I would only give it one shot, meaning, I would meet up with one guy, just for the sake of it, and then finish the website subscription.

I can't remember who emailed who first, whether Terry emailed me, or I emailed Terry. But we somehow got in touch and arranged to meet. I remember, when Sylwia and I saw Terry's photo on the web, I commented that he looked like a troll — big nose, spikey hair and a funny-looking face. I think it was more his profile description that got me to meet up with him ...

The date had been set, the preparations were underway. I lived at my sister's at the time, and I arranged to meet with Terry in our local pub, The Red Lion. I had my mobile phone on me with my sister's number on speed-dial. I worried, as I'd heard stories of girls meeting weirdos through internet dating! So my sister and my brother-in-law were instructed that if I called, even if I didn't say anything, they must come and collect me from the pub immediately.

So with a solid backup plan in place, I went to Ealing Broadway tube station to meet with Terry. I recognised him immediately. He looked just like the photo — he was wearing a leather jacket and some leather shoes that matched the jacket. I don't remember what we said to each other. I remember we went to The Red Lion, ordered drinks and the conversation was flowing. Terry turned out, thank God, not to be a freak. I texted my sister to say that she could relax.

A few buckets of Hoegaarden and a few glasses of JD & Coke later, Terry's friend turned up in the pub. I found it a bit strange that Terry felt okay with his mate coming to our first date?!?! The story was that Terry's friend, Ben, had a comedy gig at the local club, Ealing Studios, and just popped in to say 'Hi'. I was glad he only stayed for one or two drinks then quickly buggered off, as I really enjoyed my first date with Terry and wasn't keen on sharing my time with him.

We got pretty drunk that night. I invited Terry to my place. Nothing happened — as I said, we were pretty drunk. Terry ordered a taxi and went home.

So that was my one and only shot at internet dating and it turned out to be really successful, and life-changing really! We have now been happily together for 10 years (we met in March 2007), and got married in 2009. We have a child, a dog, a cat and a house. Life is good.

And now Terry ...

So this is how I remember it ... I was about a year out of a long-term relationship and only several weeks out of a ridiculous six-month fling with my 20-year-old PA from work, when I was out on a boys' night drinking with a couple of buddies — Damian Coldwell and the one-and-only Jesse Mulligan. During the night, they were telling me some hilarious stories of online dating experiences they had been having lately. (Jesse's oompa-loompa date was a particular highlight.) It was when online dating still had a real stigma of being for desperate-and-dateless types only, and was generally considered a bit uncool. I wasn't really keen at first, but eventually they convinced me to join the site they were using. It was 'mysinglefriend.com'. (I just looked it up for the first time in forever and it still exists!)

I thought that, worst-case scenario, I could maybe get some material from the dates for use on stage at some point. The concept of the site was slightly different to the norm, in that a friend of yours would write a flattering bio and post some photos of you, and then you could add a personal comment or two below the friend's comments.

This is the scandalous bit that even Ania doesn't know about yet, but I faked it and wrote my own profile, pretending to be the wife of a best friend and raving about what a great guy Terry was, and that I was perfect boyfriend material, etc. I figured it would sound better and a bit more attractive coming from a woman, I guess, and I also really wasn't keen on letting too many people know I was dipping into online dating. I'm sure I wasn't the only one to ever 'cheat' on that particular site. It was actually really easy, as I only had to set up a second email, from memory.

I went on a few dates from the site, but didn't really click with any of them. In only week two on the site, one Saturday I went on three separate dates. Lunch, dinner — and then the third one had the joy of coming to one of my stand-up gigs. She quite enjoyed being in the green room and hanging out to see the show from backstage, but she ended up getting the phone number of one of the other acts before the night ended.

Ania was probably about date five or six. I chose her profile because she looked amazing, but also she was Polish and I've always had a real thing for accents. Her profile was written by a male friend of hers (who I'm now good friends with as well) and made her out to sound like a lot of fun — into drinking games, pub lock-ins and a big fan of rugby. She was 10 years younger than me, but I sent her a message through the site, and she replied, and then this went on for a few days before we agreed to meet for a date. She wanted me to come to Ealing in London, where she lived, to meet at a pub which I remember was called The Red Lion. It was across the road from a regular comedy gig, and luckily that night Ben Hurley was doing a spot there and, just in case the date wasn't going well, I arranged for him to pop in just after his gig and make an excuse for me to leave with him.

I met her at the tube station and was absolutely smitten at first sight. Conversation flowed easily from the get-go, and she matched me drink for drink. The only thing I wasn't sure of was she was a smoker, but she was way too good-looking, and so much fun to be around, that it was never going to be a roadblock. We were both quite drunk by the time Ben arrived, and I quickly sent him on his way as the date was going so well — no need for excuses to leave early. We ended up going back to her place for a drink, where her sister had been on standby as well, to rescue Ania by coming to the pub if she got a text message saying the date was terrible. Luckily, she got the text calling her off pretty early. We exchanged numbers at the end of the night. She was the only person I had a second date with from the site — and the last person I've dated as well.

*

What strikes me about both of these tales is that, irrespective of the technology involved in getting two people in the same room, all the age-old laws of attraction apply. 'Kane' and 'Brad' picking each other out on NZDating was doubtless about symmetry and love maps, and what Kym and Dave experienced that first Saturday was chemistry, chemicals and unmistakeably love-at-first-sight. And there's Terry's love map: Ania had an accent, loved rugby and drinking — three things he consciously looked for in a lady. Ania noting that his jacket matched his shoes is a pretty clear indication that dressing properly ranks pretty high on her list of what's hot, and there's evidence of the Halo Effect working its magic — his online profile said he was 'perfect boyfriend material', sufficiently countering any perceived lack of photogenic appeal. And as much as algorithms might have played a role, there were matchmaking mates sitting over shoulders playing their traditional role, too. ('Eew' / 'Ooh'.) We're never going to take the 'human' out of human relationships.

Let's go meet a couple of people who had quite similar love maps to Terry and Ania: she admires his sartorial elegance, he's impressed with her ability to knock 'em back and retain her dignity. It's a story from 60 years ago, and it's my mum and dad.

CHAPTER 22

Old School

I SAT DOWN WITH MY PARENTS in October 2016 to talk about how they met. Little snippets of their story have found their way into family legend — that it was my mother who did the proposing, that what my father first noticed about her was her admirable bosom — but where and when and how they had courted in the 1950s was only a blurry half-story in my head. I'd never asked, and it wasn't one of those oft-told dinner party entertainments. But we'd talked about this book as I was researching it, and it made me curious about where their story started.

It is not strictly a great 'How We Met' story: nothing wildly serendipitous, no instant fireworks — the opposite really. But what I love about this is that it's a snapshot of an era. Post-war young women and men beginning to feel free and hopeful again, but not yet showing much of an appetite for eschewing social conventions, as the hippies would in the decade that followed. A particular moment in time.

I also love it because it was one of the last big talks the three of us had. Dad died exactly three months to the day after I made this recording. It is a strange and lovely thing to hear his voice on the tape with his idiosyncratic turns of phrase — he seemed to know a lot of 'top-class men' in the 1950s, and almost none of the other kind. Listening back to it, I also realise it is the inverse of an election debate with Mike Hosking, Bill English and Jacinda Ardern: Mother and I both interrupt him quite often, and at times he can barely get a word in. I'd hate anyone to do one of those 'minutes spoken / number of interruptions' graphs on us A'Court ladies.

My father was a very private man, so it was inordinately good of both of them to let me do this …

In 1951, **John A'Court** was 22 years old and working at the Sander Tie Company on Dixon Street in Wellington. He had started working there in 1947 straight after he'd left school. Dad would go on to spend his whole career in clothing manufacturing, but it didn't start out as his choice. His father had simply come home one day and said, 'I've got you a job. You're going to start there on Monday.' No discussion. Dad's father had heard around the traps that Waldo Zander was looking for a young apprentice, and had gone ahead and arranged it — although not before doing due diligence on Sander Ties. My grandfather worked for the Inland Revenue

Department. 'What he did say to me — I'll never forget this — he said, "I've had a look at their books," and he said, "They're a good company."' I'm fairly certain it was highly illegal for an IRD employee to go snooping around in someone's tax records for personal reasons. 'Oh, yes,' Dad says. 'That was unlike my father back then.' Still, his illegally acquired intelligence proved to be correct: Waldo Zander is one of Dad's most esteemed 'top-class men'.

By 1951, Dad had risen to the role of manager with 15 staff. Outside work, he was passionate about sport and fitness — he'd been a damn fine athlete as a schoolboy at Wellington College, and now he was regularly working out at the YMCA on Willis Street. These days, he says, there are gyms all over the place, but back then there was pretty much just the Y. To use the weights room, you had to go and get the key from reception. 'And it turned out the person at the desk was Donna.' My mother volunteers that at that point she has just turned 17. 'You were a child!' I say. 'I *was* a child. I didn't go out with him then, but that was where we met.'

In 1951, **Donna Pengelly** was working at the YMCA while studying part-time at Victoria University, aiming to fill in a year before she was old enough to go to Teachers Training College. She'd nip out from behind reception and up the hill to attend lectures in English, psychology and French.

'Did you quite like the look of her?' I ask him, and there's a flicker of a smile. 'I did.' It took him a year, my mother says, to ask her out, although he is surprised to think it was that long. Casting his mind back, he says he thought she might make the first move. 'I was hoping that she'd ring me up. Nothing occurred for quite a long time.' She is firm that this was not how things worked. 'Young ladies didn't ring young gentlemen up in those days. It was the other way around. You waited and waited forever. You could be an old maid before you'd ring up a chap.'

They did, however, strike up conversations at the YMCA front desk when he came by. They both remember him telling her a story about being given the job of transporting his sister Alma's wedding cake to the reception in the back of his car — a cake heavily decorated with bridge work, much of which was broken by the time he got to the wedding breakfast. They both seemed to find that amusing, then and now.

But it wasn't until 1952 that they saw each other outside the gym. 'We happened to both be at the Majestic Cabaret, where we spent a lot of time in our young days,' my mother says. 'It was really quite beautiful, with the double staircase and everybody dressed to go there and so on.' It was the fashion that men wore dinner suits, women wore ballet-length gowns with floaty underskirts — my mother's description of the Majestic paints a picture of elegance, and it is backed up by photographs they have of the time. 'Father was with another party, and I was with another party, but he came and asked me to dance and sort of muscled in and said, would I meet him for coffee the next day at the California Coffee Bar down the road … I said yes. They say there are no free lunches, but there was that day.'

There is a photograph of them taken in January 1954 that I adore: the two of them waiting for a visit from a young Queen Elizabeth outside the Wellington Town Hall, eating plums from a paper bag. He's all cheekbones and long eyelashes, she's all dimples with sparkly eyes. By that time, my mother says, they were going out quite regularly, but still not 'a couple' — they went out with other people, too. 'I can remember one year around that time, I went to 13 balls with 11 different partners. That was the way that you did it. People didn't seem to turn into couples quite so quickly in those days. It was much more of a mating dance.' I say this sounds like the American style of dating, which my generation didn't do — we were all about falling into bed of an evening and waking up in the morning to start finding out who they were. None of that nonsense in their set. Sure, if you went out with someone for an evening you'd feel an obligation to be 'partnered' on the dance floor and at the table, but that didn't mean he was Your Partner. Nope, you'd be off out to lunch the next day with someone else, and there'd be another chap for a ball or the Majestic Cabaret on Friday night.

When did they decide they were going out together, then? Neither of them are exactly sure, but it was after the Queen and the plums. 'It's not necessarily a day that you decide it, just somewhere along the line,' she says, 'the side issues fell away and there was just the two of you really.' She points out that she was still very young: when they married in 1955, she was a few weeks shy of turning 21.

I ask for the proposal story from 1954 and, as they launch into it, you can hear on the recording that our conversation is accompanied by the sound of me refilling everyone's wine glasses. This is entirely appropriate. Because as glamorous and elegant as these evenings were at the Majestic Cabaret on Willis Street (and the balls, and the Naval events they attended after my father was commissioned in the Reserve — my mother always quite liked being saluted), we need to point out that none of these places were licensed to sell booze. Which did not mean everyone was sober. Not at all. It meant that in places like the Majestic, or up the top of the cable car at The Skyline, you might nip in during the day and secrete your bottles of liquor up the mock-chimneys — designed, one might imagine, for exactly that purpose. Either that, or the lady would slip a bottle of something up the sleeve of her bell-sleeved coat on the way to the venue, and place the bottle carefully under the table. Tumblers would be supplied by management (ostensibly for water, but no one seems clear about whether water was actually served), and you would fill said tumblers with the booze you'd snuck in. The police would amble about during the course of the evening, keeping an eye out with only occasional success.

My parents were up at The Skyline one night when it was raided and it all ended up in the newspaper. 'It was a big deal,' my father says. 'Yes,' my mother says, 'the chef was absolutely devastated, because they took his cooking liqueurs for the flambé. Even the sherry for the trifle — the police took that as well.'

My mother's *modus operandi* was to put a half-bottle of whisky up one sleeve for Dad, and a half-bottle of brandy up the other sleeve for herself. 'We shouldn't mention it perhaps,' my father, ever the gentleman, says, 'but the fact is Donna would drink the brandy and I would drink the scotch and she would finish before I did.' 'Then I'd help him finish the scotch,' my mother says cheerfully. 'Your father found that quite admirable, I think.' I agree that the ability to hold your liquor is very attractive on a lady. 'A quite *young* lady,' my mother emphasises. 'It's astonishing, really,' Dad says, still clearly impressed.

This explains Dad's response when, on the day of another sister's wedding — his youngest sister, Iris, this time — they were at the Majestic Cabaret after the festivities and my mother said to him, 'I'd quite like to marry you.' First words out of his mouth were, 'You've been drinking, haven't you?' Had you, I ask? 'Yes, but I'm a woman of my word.' Dad then stepped out for a moment with his best pal, Ian, and told him, 'Miss Pengelly's asked me to marry her.' Ian said something along the lines of 'Crikey', indicating that John A'Court was a pretty lucky dude. He'd been waiting for her to make the first move, remember, back at the YMCA, and now she had.

They were officially engaged on 17 April 1954, and married on 5 March 1955. I ask them to tell me what it is they found attractive about each other. Dad begins diffidently, trying to avoid references to Mother's admirable bosom, and comes up with this: 'I was certainly attracted, but I find it hard to say what it was. It seemed to me that this was a person that I could talk to, and she looked pretty attractive and … I don't know.'

My mother is more certain, and quotes an old family friend. 'Dear old Jessie Jean Kidd used to say, "Oh, chemistry, Donna! That's what happens. It's chemistry and there's no stopping it!" I think probably there is always something quite unexplainable, isn't there, about why two people should choose to throw in their lot together? I really think that there is just some kind of spark there. John, of course, was very good company and very lively company. He was always the one dancing on the tables and hanging off the chandeliers.' He was also, she says, what they called in those days a 'groppy' dresser — beautiful suits, silk ties, immaculate shirts. He was, after all, in the business. 'We wore hats in those days,' he says, with a tone that suggests all men still should.

He was also delighted by my mother's theatre friends. By this time, theatre was a big part of her life, both as an actor and behind the scenes. When Dad saw her on stage at the Concert Chamber, it was possibly the first play he'd ever been to. He enjoyed this theatre thing so much that he would even go with her to rehearsals. Her thespian friends were different from the people he'd known at school or from his family's church. 'These other people that Donna knew were very entertaining. I found them really great fun to be with,' Dad says. 'Many gay people. We didn't know too much about gay people in those days.' Quite. This was 30 years before Homosexual Law Reform, when gay men had to keep their sexuality hidden in public for fear of arrest and imprisonment. But not in private — not at the theatre and its after-parties, and not at my parents' house.

Here's the bit that will tick off millennials: in between getting engaged and getting married, Dad bought a house. We work through the numbers. The house cost £1200; Dad was earning about £800 a year; and he took out a five-year mortgage. Sure, it was a two-bedroom starter home on the side of a steep hill in Wellington's windswept Wilton, but it was also *theirs*. Dad moved in before Christmas in 1954, built steps, put some chooks in around the back, got the place ready. 'You didn't move in?' I ask my mother. 'Heavens no!' she says with mock horror. 'What are you suggesting?' She moved in after the wedding. In today's terms, it would be like someone on the average wage being able to buy a house for about $80,000. I didn't have the heart to ask them whether they also ate smashed avocado at brunches in town.

A little starter home, but perfect for parties with its big open living area. 'Oh, it was,' my mother says. 'At two o'clock in the morning, it really sang!' After one of her plays, they'd all repair to the Savage Club Hall, and when they were turfed out at closing time they'd head up to John and Donna's to keep the party going until 5am. They had only one neighbour — an old couple, Dad says. 'Well, we thought they were an old couple. I don't know how old they were really.' 'They were about 40,' Mother says. Dad says, 'They were lovely people, but they thought that we were absolutely scandalous.'

The wheelbarrow wouldn't have helped. As I say, the house was high up on the side of a hill, and the steps down could be treacherous for guests in the early dawn. 'We used to wheel them down in a wheelbarrow,' Dad says, 'the ones that couldn't walk.'

My mother notes that, of Dad's original gang of friends, all of them married and never divorced. She puts that down to this long mating dance — that they knew each other well before they made that commitment. She is not suggesting, she says, that people didn't have sex before marriage or didn't have random sex, and she's not even suggesting it was a moral thing. It was that you didn't settle down with someone, didn't marry them, until you knew them well.

'You knew a circle of people and you tended to go out with them and get to know them perhaps. Suddenly somebody that you hadn't thought too much of for 18 months, you'd think, "Oh, he's really very nice. Yes."'

*

My parents were five weeks short of their sixty-second wedding anniversary when my father died. He had a stroke on New Year's Eve and was in hospital for all of January 2017. Every day when I visited, he'd open his eyes and say, 'Hello, my darling,' momentarily alert and pleased. Sometimes he'd go into long, convoluted stories about his delusions (from the drugs and the effects of the stroke), and then he'd suddenly look at me hard with clear eyes and say, as though he'd only just seen me, 'You doing okay, 'Chèle?' And I'd think, he can see I'm worried, or sad, or distressed, or just lying to him about how he was, as you do when people are mortally ill. And I'd say, 'I'm good, Dad.' And he'd nod, unconvinced, but accepting of being complicit in our ruse.

I was away on a short comedy tour with my husband, Jeremy, and our friend from the previous chapter, Terry, when I got a call from Mother saying I needed to come back. We'd just left Stewart Island and were heading for Te Anau. I got the first flight out of Queenstown the next day, picked up my mother, and arrived at his bedside around 5.30pm. He was unconscious. We talked to him, and held his hand. As we left, I said, 'It's okay, Dad. I love you. You can let go.' This was at 6.22pm — I know this because as we walked out of the hospital, Jeremy rang so the time is recorded on my phone. My mother and I drove to the supermarket to pick up dinner, and, as we were driving home, my phone rang again. It was the nurse on his ward to say that Dad had died at 6.25pm. Once he knew that I was there to be with my mother and help her do all the things that needed to be done after he'd gone, he waited until we left the room to slip away. It seems to me that this was a very strong thing to do.

My parents and I have shared a roof since 1995: their home is on the ground floor; mine is upstairs. Different front doors. Dad had left our house for the last time on the morning of New Year's Eve in an ambulance with my mother. I stayed behind for a bit to tidy up. Shortly after the ambulance drove away, my cat Satchmo caught a blackbird and placed it neatly on my parents' doorstep. Daytime bird-hunts are rare. A month later, on the night my father died, Satchmo brought a live blackbird into my bedroom and sat beside it patiently, waiting for me to wake up. I took the bird outside and let it go. The next evening, at 10pm, he brought in a large live rat and delivered it to me in the living room. He knew we needed comforting, so he was bringing gifts. The birds hadn't been a success. He was exploring other options. Weeks later, when I bring Dad's ashes home, I leave the box overnight in the living room. When I get up in the morning, Satchmo is asleep, wrapped around the box.

I can only tell you these things because I wrote them down at the time. I wouldn't have remembered them otherwise. It is as Professor Addis says: in moments of stress, your brain is so overloaded with thoughts and emotions and events, some of the memories don't get properly recorded in your brain-office. If I look at my diary for January and February 2017 and see the things I did — the appointments, the errands, the tasks to do and done — all I can think is, 'Really? Did I?' It's not just new memories that get lost — for weeks I had trouble remembering people's names, and finding nouns, and dealing with spatial things like navigating my way from one suburb to another in the car. Hippocampus overload.

So I like it that I wrote those things down about Satchmo — little markers for significant days, and the kindness and empathy of a cat. 'Meaning-making', as Professor Addis called it. Or as I've always thought of it, creating little stories to find order in the chaos.

*

One of the first things you do when someone dies is go digging around in your brain for the memories you want to share at their funeral.

Being a child is our first role, the first person we are in the world. While your parents are there — even when you've reached the place where you're feeding them ice cream on a teaspoon — you can still escape to being their child, and rest your head on their shoulder. I had thought I understood grief before Dad died, but I suddenly felt like I needed to apologise to anyone who had lost a parent, for only showing them an ordinary amount of sympathy.

Because when you lose a parent, you lose a vital person from your very first story. It took a month before I could articulate this, and it was in an email to one of my favourite English teachers from high school. Anthony Dreaver had written to me to say he was sorry to hear my father had died, that he had been 'such a decent chap, gentle and thoughtful' and that he knew Dad had been proud of me, 'his challenging but delightful daughter'. It is honestly the nicest thing anyone has ever said.

I told Mr Dreaver (he will always be 'Mr Dreaver' in my head) that what I was feeling most was this: that the person Dad was with me was different from his other selves. (And of course the person he was with Mother, and with my brother Stephen, was also unique to them.) He was particularly soft and gentle with me — bewildered by me sometimes, but never judgemental. I think I was a curiosity, but he didn't wish that I was different. And so of course, just as he was a particular version of himself with me, the person I was with him was different from my other selves. And that's where the grief lives: that the part of me that is my father's daughter doesn't get to come out and play now. I told Mr Dreaver that I don't know what happens to her, but I will work it out over time.

At my father's funeral, my brother and I found stories that made us children again. My brother told a story from our childhood that I had forgotten for more than 40 years — about coming home from a long trip, us still in the car, our dad going in through the side door of the garage to open the big door. It had three round windows in it at a grown person's head height. Dad spent several minutes popping his head up at each window with a daft look on his face, while we tried to guess which window he'd appear at next. Stephen's story made me laugh harder than you possibly should at a funeral. It was glorious.

My parents were both terrific dancers and my mother has already mentioned that Dad had a penchant for 'swinging from chandeliers' and literally dancing on tables. This continued when we were kids, although it was a side of him we rarely saw at home. For his funeral, I told the story of one notable evening when my parents had gone out to a house-warming at a friend's place and Dad had danced on their brand-new dining table and broken it. I remember being shocked that my serious, sensible father could do such a thing, and then intrigued that he didn't seem at all remorseful. I think he and I were both quite proud of the whole affair. I have made a promise to honour his memory by dancing on tables every chance I get.

CHAPTER 23

'Let's Go to Paris'

WHEN YOU READ MY PARENTS' story of courting in the 1950s, you might assume that falling in love was a steady and sedate thing in the olden days. Are you mad? This story is our oldest tale. It's from the 1930s and could easily have been placed in Chapter 14: 'When Love Makes You Do Crazy Things', but I wanted to put it here as a contrast to the story that came before.

Frank was born in 1909; Cicely in 1913. They are no longer with us, so this is their love story written by their daughter, Frances Denz. It features Selwyn Toogood, the All Blacks, and science-lab gin.

*

*My mum, **Cicely Render**, and my dad, **Frank Denz**,*
both lived in Wellington. The year they met was 1934.
Frank had run away from his abusive father, a

Pākehā railway worker, to go to Victoria University to get his MSc. His Māori mother had died when he was a child, as a result of an abortion.

Cicely was born in Britain and came to New Zealand when she was 10, with her very enterprising mother and compliant and kindly father. As a young adult she still lived with her family in Roseneath. She was a secretary/typist at AMP. She seems to have had a reasonably active social life for those times.

When Frank received his MSc he decided to leave New Zealand for London to do medicine. This was a huge venture, as he had no backing, no resources and no money, only innocence and an absolute desire to be a doctor. Four days before his departure, he held a leaving party at his digs near the Bolton Street Cemetery. As no one had any money, and bought alcohol was a luxury, he prepared a large amount of gin in the university lab, which he took to the house in lab flasks.

Cicely was invited to the party by someone she later described as a large young man with a booming voice who finished up running quizzes on TV. She couldn't remember his name. It will have been Selwyn Toogood. She walked into the party on his arm, to stop abruptly when she saw a young man pouring gin from a lab flask on the other side of the room. She abandoned her partner, and walked over to Frank, who looked deeply into her eyes, handed her a gin, put his arm around her, and never let her go all evening. It was instant love.

At the end of the evening he walked her home to Roseneath, and arranged to meet her after work the following day. Loaded with fish and chips and more gin, they climbed up to the Bolton Street Cemetery again, where, as Mum later commented, 'they did their courting'. The old roses on the graves were blooming and he threaded her long dark hair with Albéric Barbier *and* Félicité et Perpétue, *two roses which are still there today. They did the same the next two evenings, until Dad sailed away, with promises of everlasting love.*

Mum spent the next year saving literally every penny she could. She stopped using the tram to and from work, but walked, although she ruefully commented that the savings were marginal as the cost in shoe leather was very high. Eventually, however, she had saved enough to get on a boat to England. By all accounts it was a great trip, as there were only three unattached girls and the entire 1935 All Black team. Mum never told me whether she considered herself one of the three unattached girls!

When she arrived in England, Dad met her on the wharf and cheerfully asked her if she had any money as he was down to his last pound. They sat in a teashop sharing a cup of tea (to save money), and worked out that they had enough money to pay for either an immediate wedding and no honeymoon plus the fare to London, or to delay the wedding and go on their honeymoon to Paris and get married when they got back. Sleeping with someone before you got married was still a big taboo, but Mum excitedly said, 'Let's go to Paris', so they went down to the next wharf for the ferry to France.

Financially, the next few years were tough. Mum worked as a secretary, and paid Dad's fees. Along the way he had a breakdown and asked for time to pay, to be told firmly that 'a gentleman can always pay his debts'. As a young colonial Māori boy he was treated appallingly, and they were frequently hungry, and sometimes doing what is now known as 'couch-surfing', but he got his degree, and when war broke out he finished up as a major in the British Army.

When he died in 1960, aged 50, my mother was devastated, and never really recovered. She lost her identity. She had always called herself 'Frank's wife', and now there was no Frank.

*

Cicely lived for another 43 years — she died in 2003, one day before her ninetieth birthday. Frances loves their tale. 'I always thought it was so romantic, and quite hard to fathom as my mother was quite prosaic!' Which is another reason I love stories like this — that they show us those other 'selves' each of us has, and gather us all in closer.

CHAPTER 24

Wisdom: What Have They Learned?

AT THE END OF EVERY INTERVIEW, I'd keep the recorder going and ask couples for their relationship advice: hot takes and top reckons for love and longevity. I always felt like a dick asking the question, but the answers made it worth it. 'Like a dick', because none of these lovely people ever presented themselves as relationship experts, or holders of the key to universal happiness, or privy to the secret of success for anyone but themselves, so it felt cheeky to suddenly cast them in that role. But 'worth it' because they really did have things to say — both practical and philosophical — about making relationships work. Let's make a list.

1. Let go of the little things — the dumb stuff and small irritations. This was noted as an observation about themselves, rather than as an order to everyone else: a process of evolution, not a goal they'd set. Over the four decades Belynda has been with Martin, she says she's become much less bothered by minor issues, and has learned to let go of old wounds. (Though I reckon she'd still like her Queen's Scout Award.) Faye says the same — that she could be 'difficult' in the beginning, but she's more relaxed now. And with everyone there is a sense that, after a decade or three, you've got a pretty good handle on what matters and what doesn't. What matters? These words came up every time: kindness, compromise and mutual respect. And then, after you've let go of the little things ...

2. Notice the little things — the small kindnesses and loving gestures. No matter how busy their lives are, Martin will find a moment to phone Belynda every day to see how she is, check in with her — even more so since the day they lost each other during the Christchurch earthquakes. For lots of couples, it's about keeping someone fed. Māwera is an obvious example, with her drive to fatten Dave up so he would look like someone who was loved, but there are more: Roger delivering roast vegetable paninis to Briony when she was up to her eyeballs with the opening of Te Papa; Warren cooking a degustation for Faye while she read a book; and Sally told me she thinks her relationship with Neil works because 'he rescues me, I feed him'. It doesn't have to be food (though food turns up a lot), but it is a signifier that you are satisfying one of those primal needs. When my Great-aunt Ruth was sitting on the back porch of an evening in Napier, my Great-uncle Frank used to come outside with her cardigan so she didn't get chilly. I've always thought of that as a supremely romantic gesture. Food, warmth and making sure the other one of you is safe.

3. Time together. All of our couples genuinely enjoy each other's company. Neil and Sally live large portions of their life in a house-bus so they can be together even when he's working out of town. Elizabeth and Tom don't like to let each other out of their sight, and have arranged their lives to be close to Amber. Tim loves it that Jane has stopped working full-time so that they can spontaneously take off together on one of his business trips. Sometimes, just for fun, they'll go camping in their own living room and they use their outdoor shower. They haven't had a TV for years — they'd rather hang out together and talk.

4. Time apart. Jane says she won't let Tim retire until he's 85, because she needs to have time on her own as well. Māwera occasionally sends Dave off 'to kill something' so she feels less inclined to kill him. Roger has a motorbike and Briony's not always on the back of it. Soraya sings barbershop or watches *The*

Bachelor upstairs while Jim does his artwork or watches Netflix downstairs (he can't stand barbershop or *The Bachelor*). If he stays up very late, he might sleep in the spare room, although he says he's just as likely to slip into bed and hug her at 3am. All the couples have some separate (sometimes conflicting) interests.

5. Fight with each other. Soraya and Jim love a good ding-dong. Faye and Warren used to. Briony mentions at one point that marriages have their 'moments', and everyone makes some kind of reference to 'moments' of their own. Personally, I've always thought that if a couple never fights, one of them must be spineless. No one seriously offered up the old adage of 'never go to bed angry' — in fact, when I was talking with Maria and Patrick, I mentioned that I quite like the occasional angry-sleep in the spare room. They don't do shouty-fights: Maria came from a house with a lot of violence and fighting, and she will do anything to avoid that; and Patrick says that as the youngest of six children, by the time he came along his parents seemed to have resolved everything — certainly no raised voices he can recall — though that has its own problems, because it meant he freaked out the first time someone raised a voice in one of his earlier relationships. He didn't see how that could possibly work, and bailed. He's had to learn that it is okay to disagree and work things through. Maria says they do a little bit of snapping and sulking. 'I snap, and she sulks,' Patrick says, which we agree is a fair division of labour. We also agree that apologies are important — those genuine ones where you apologise for what you did or said, not the ones where you say you're sorry they took it badly.

6. Fight on the same side. Teaming up together to go into battle is a bonding thing. We saw that with Māwera and Dave and his fight for custody of his kids; and to some extent with Elizabeth and Tom supporting each other through his difficulties with his first family, now that he has a second. Lots of couples talk about facing shared challenges: Sally and Neil with their time in a cult-like church, Tim and Jane being told they'd never make it 40 years ago, Soraya and Jim both coping with the death of a parent, Belynda and Martin dealing with family illnesses and earthquakes. All those moments of steadying each other while the ground is shaking under you can weave you closer.

7. Romance — yeah, nah. It really struck me that no one ever described themselves as a romantic couple. In fact, it was clearer than that: everyone I asked said they were 'not romantic'. The traditional view of romance — hearts and flowers, grand gestures, flashmob proposals, poetry, skywriting, a mariachi band at your restaurant table — no one was into it. Not in a sneering way; people were almost apologetic that they didn't do the things we often think of as 'romantic'. But. Every couple celebrates their relationship at least once a year with an anniversary; often twice — the meeting and the wedding, if there was one. (And if it's not a date, as with Maria and Patrick, it's a *place*.) And in between those dates, they also tell their story. So to be honest, when they show me the treasure box with its inscription, or tell me how sad they were when the building they first met in was demolished, or describe sitting up at night making bunting for their wedding, or reveal their tattoos, or list the things they rescued from their apartment while they searched for their partner in the ruins, or show me the candle they had at their wedding and light up again every year, and then tell me they are 'not romantic', I call bullshit.

8. Friendship — hell, yeah. And courting and dating. We hear frequent recommendations for getting to know each other well before getting into bed. Although falling into bed (or a shower block, same difference) and then dating works, too — the order doesn't appear to be crucial. Just some period of sex being out of the equation seems to lead to other delights. Three months of phone calls between Tom and Elizabeth; several months of fish'n'chips on the beach for Declan and Maeve; chatting in the living room while the boyfriend put chilli in everything at the other end of the house for Patrick and Maria; three years of dancing with and around each other for my parents; a decade-and-a-half of being pals for Briony and Roger ... Those long courtships might have been imposed by circumstance, but everyone who experienced them relished the experience of being friends before (or after, and then before again) becoming lovers.

9. Soulmaking. Given the opportunity, everyone will describe their partner as someone who helps make them 'a better person'. One of my favourite times I asked my dick-question ('What relationship advice would you give?') was with Maria and Patrick. Maria started with: 'It's that soulmaking idea that suggests you are attracted to someone' — and they say it simultaneously — 'for a *reason*.'

They subscribe to the Jungian concept that we are all either in the process of becoming, or striving to become, our mature selves. Evolving, refining who we are by examining ourselves — the conscious and unconscious parts of who we are, how we think, how we see ourselves in the world. Long-term relationships are one of the main ways we are forced to grow into ourselves, because when you're with someone for many years, bonded closely to them, there is nowhere to hide: all that unconscious stuff is going to come out over time and will need to be examined. And perhaps when you see something in your partner you don't like it's because you have it in yourself. (It's not you, it's me.) Their faults or mistakes or flaws are the ones you need to deal with in yourself.

Which means you are drawn to someone who 'completes' you in the sense that they challenge you to understand yourself better. Which might be uncomfortable at times, and will require open, honest communication.

'It is the idea of knocking each other's edges off, and making a thing together that is greater than you are on your own ... It is a mystery, what draws you together,' Maria says, and Patrick adds: 'It's God's sweet mystery, really, isn't it? The Fates haven't put you together to make you dumb and happy. It's about growing. It's a soulmaking business.'

10. Being run out of town by the cops. I just want to chuck this in here, because I have been tickled by those two separate stories of Tim Sandbrook in Dannevirke, 1977, and Sally Hunter in Bulls, 1971, looking like they were going off the rails and it being suggested by the local constabulary that it might be wise for them to move on and start afresh. Which meant Tim could meet Jane in Hamilton, and Sally took a break in Australia before coming back to meet Neil in Palmerston North. If ever there was an argument for a return to properly funded small-town community policing, this is it.

CHAPTER 25

What Have We Learned?

SINCE THAT DINNER with Ian and Clare in Rarotonga — the night on the beach with oceans of booze and terrific company and live music and the question that started it all — I've talked to vast numbers of couples about they how met. Randomly at dinners, in bars and office corridors, and specifically with meetings and Skyping and emails. Forty-two stories have made it into this book — a handful of them are from people I knew a little, or whose friends I knew, but most of them were complete strangers when we began. I'd fall in love with each couple as I wrote about them — finish a chapter and be sorry to see them go — and then get all hot and frothy over the next pair. 'I love your story, it's my favourite!' I'd tell everyone, and mean it.

I have been fickle, then, but they haven't, bless them. I was worried at the start that, during this process — almost three years from idea to bookshelf — people might break up, and break my heart a bit along with their own. I couldn't bear the idea of capturing someone's story and then watching it float away, plus I was terrified that turning up in a book about falling in love might somehow jinx it for them. But it didn't ever happen, and I am thrilled about that for them and us.

Which all by itself suggests that my overarching thesis might be pretty bang on. That having a great 'How We Met' story gives people a sense of belonging to each other and helps bind them firmly together. Somewhere during the process, I began to think of it as a microcosm of that huge idea of whakapapa: that knowing your history, mapping your roots, recounting your legends and shared stories are ways not only of *showing* connections, but of reinforcing them. It works for whānau, hapū and iwi, and I really believe it works for couples, too.

So your story holds you together during the challenging times, and also — in the retelling — can take you back to those first memories and reignite the emotions and passion. But which comes first: the great story, or the great relationship? Relationship therapist Sara Chatwin said it was both: a bit of magic at the start sets you on your path; and if you stay on your path together, that first meeting seems even more magical.

Neuroscientist Professor Donna Rose Addis (I'm pulling out all the big guns now) agrees. She says there is a 'bi-directional relationship' between our memories and our present self. The mood of the relationship will colour how we tell the story; and also the story sets the tone for the relationship. Because memory, remember (yes, I know what I just did there), is not about record-keeping. It is about reconstructing your past in a way that supports who we feel we are in the present. And if the memory involves two people, then together we will choose the memories that support who we are as a couple.

Bi-directional between present and past, and also between present and future. Once we have reconstructed this lovely story about ourselves, it makes it easier, Donna Rose says, to then go on to imagine a positive future for us. 'It leads really naturally into imagining where you're going together. If you can do that together, you would probably then find that you have much richer imaginings. That's going to make you solidify where you're going as well.' So sitting in the present, savouring a great story from the past, helps create a clearer, brighter future. You are all very welcome.

Somewhere between the research and the writing, a curious mind asked if there was anything we could say about the people who have great 'How We Met' stories. Do they have anything in common? Unless I've missed something, they have nothing in common in terms of age (34 to 96), ethnicity, sexual orientation, socio-economic class, belief system, geography or even personality type. Sure, someone in each couple had to be outgoing enough to contact me and agree to a chat, but I swear they weren't a bunch of show ponies — there was diffidence and shyness mixed in with wanting to tell a story that they treasured. Not all genders are represented — I wasn't able to entice any transgender or non-binary people into the book — so I acknowledge that gap and wish it was otherwise.

But here is what all of the couples in this book *do* have in common. They all have:

(a) a story about how they met, that
(b) they like to tell, and by telling it they
(c) rekindle those first feelings again, which
(d) helps keep them together when life gets in the way,
and
(e) makes it possible to imagine a happy future, which
(f) makes a happy future possible.

Which is fabulous for them, and useful, and precious. But what if you, Dear Reader, don't have a great 'How We Met' story? What special alchemy can you use to glue yourself to your One In Particular? Let's have one last story — not of 'how we met', but of 'how I met his friends'.

CHAPTER 26

How I Met His Friends

JEREMY AND I DON'T have a great 'How We Met' story. I mean, it's all right, and I could flossy it up and say, 'The first time I saw him it was like he was the most significant person in the room, and he was surrounded by a golden light, and there was music.' By which I mean we met at work — at The Classic comedy club. He was standing onstage under a spotlight with his guitar, performing a solo comedy song. So, yeah. Actual golden light, literally playing music.

The truth is, we noticed each other, noticed each other noticing each other, didn't do anything about it apart from some quite witty flirting (we were both in other relationships at the time), he went overseas for a year, came back, and eventually on the night before his birthday, near the end of 1999, I kissed him. Quite hard. It did the trick. Three months later we were, as Wai, the barman at The Classic so eloquently put it, 'going round together'.

At dinner parties, if anyone asks 'How did you two meet?', we say 'At work', and everyone says 'Of course', and thinks up another topic. But there is a story I really like that does, for me, the same things that this book-full of stories does for other couples. It goes like this.

It is mid-winter 2000 and Jeremy and I have travelled to Dunedin to do a comedy show together. We've been 'going round' a few months, and Jeremy tells me that, while we're in Dunedin, he wants to introduce me to his best friend and old flatmate, Patrick. They'd known each other for years, had done a lot of theatre together at The Fortune and at Allen Hall, and I had already been regaled with stories of their grand adventures and wild misdeeds. Patrick is clearly someone Jeremy greatly admires and respects, and — you know how it goes — you can't help feeling that when you meet your new boyfriend's old friends it is going to matter that you get on. There might even be a test. I was really hoping he would like me.

It is arranged that we will meet the afternoon before the gig at The Woolshed bar on Moray Place, just down from the Octagon. There will be Patrick and some other old friends, but it is Patrick who really matters. Best pals. I know it was winter, because I remember there was a fireplace with a roaring fire, and when I arrived I needed to stop briefly to take off layers of coat, scarf and hat. I was also taking a moment to tidy myself up before meeting this Patrick — Jeremy walked on ahead to where he could see a bunch of his mates by the fire, Patrick presumably among them. Suddenly, from the other direction, someone threw their arms around me and enveloped me in a quite sturdy bear-hug. And, oh my God, it was my old friend, Paddy! Paddy and I hadn't seen each other for a while — in 1990 we'd played Theatresports together and done some touring, and there had been more than one raucous night with Paddy and also Stayci, another touring comrade. At the end of a tour, all three of us had crashed together in Paddy's bed in Dunedin after dancing ourselves into some kind of oblivion to Terence Trent Darby. If I'm not entirely mistaken, Stayci had belted out the opening lyrics to 'Dance Little Sister' — 'Get up outta your rocking chair, Grandma!' — while standing on an actual rocking chair in Paddy's flat. She's pretty spectacular, that Stayci. Has the balance of a cat. Paddy is spectacular, too. Over cask wine and God knows what else, we had dreamed up superhero names for each other and promptly forgotten them the next day. It is one of the great tragedies of the 1990s that we hadn't thought to write them down at the time — they were gone from our heads by morning, replaced by hangovers. They had been *perfect* names. I am reasonably certain that mine was Gumption Girl (no particular superpowers apart from the ability to fly and a high level of pluck), but I can't tell you now if that was really it, or if I've convinced myself of that retrospectively. But Stayci and Paddy's names were entirely soluble in alcohol. It was, and is, a tremendous loss, and one of the reasons I always carry a notebook now.

So, there I am at The Woolshed with the fabulous Paddy squeezing the breath out of me, and we're saying hello and I'm starting to explain I'm there to meet my boyfriend's buddy, Patrick, and I should probably do that but then could we please have a drink? And eventually it dawns on me (and on Jeremy, who is watching this from over by the fireplace and had no idea until now) that his friend Patrick is my friend Paddy, and we are probably all going to get on like a house on fire. And we do.

And then there's Stayci, of the Theatresports tour and the rocking chair and Paddy's crowded bed. She is the same Stayci from Chapter 17 — 'Don't I Know You From Somewhere?' — (oo er, spooky), who I certainly knew by 1990, and who Jeremy must have met around the same time, but this happened entirely separately. In that earlier chapter, when Stayci describes how she first met her partner, Lucy, in Wellington, she says how generous Lucy was to give up her room to make space for Stayci and 'two other feral Dunedinites' to crash in while they were in town, under instruction from their mutual friend Sean. The two other feral Dunedinites were … Correct — Paddy and

Jeremy. And Sean is Paddy's ex-boyfriend. You may have to draw yourself a diagram to keep up.

Let's throw on one more little layer: I wanted to check the date that Lucy, Stayci, Jeremy and I had randomly discovered we were all in Italy and so met up in Florence at Piazza Santo Spirito, the night they told me their 'How We Met' story. It was 18 June 2016. Which I see, as I look in my diary, is also Paddy's birthday. Gifts all round.

Here's what I am saying: that you can find these stories if you look for them, and they can bring you huge amounts of joy, like this one does for me, and all these stories do for the people who star in them. It might be an engagement ring fumble at Yankee Stadium, or falling down a hole in a kebab shop, or a truly memorable wedding — that's what those moments are for. For retelling and savouring.

One of the things I've been most thrilled to learn is how we encode and retrieve memory — that our brain holds all those boxes filled with details, and we can dig around in them and find all sorts of treasures, even ones we thought might have been lost. (I'm going to keep searching for those superhero names, goddamn it.)

Remember Sally and Neil who had 'had words' the day we met, which meant their story was told without all of the sparkle it might have had on another, different day? The semantic version, rather than the episodic version unfolding in their brain with colour and magic. A year later, Sally sent me this astonishing collection of memories she had been able to unearth in the time since.

> *I've been thinking a lot about mine and Neil's getting together and longevity, how miraculous it actually is. It wasn't just his long hair I loved (although in those times the coolest boyfriends had to have long hair or an Afro). Neil also wore the coolest clothes and had some great albums.*
>
> *Except, he always wore the same clothes: a checked Wrangler shirt and flared Levis. I couldn't understand why sometimes, though, his shirt and jeans were loose and other times tight, and sometimes just right. It wasn't until I moved in with him that I saw he had three different sizes of the same outfit. Why? Because a menswear shop had them hanging on display outside on coat hangers, and forgot to bring them in when they closed. He had taken them all home.*
>
> *It also turned out that the* Deep Purple *and* Led Zeppelin IV *albums had been left behind by another flatmate. Neil confessed years later that he hates hard rock. I've remembered, too, that when we were driving*

and found it hard to choose music for us both (Neil went thru a Yanni stage, ugh!), I got my double Pink Floyd The Wall *CD (the cover was the title graffitied on a wall) and used a black felt to add, 'with Yanni' under it. We played it all the way to Auckland, and he loved it. 'Real music,' he said ... Dumb stuff coming back to me that I should tell my kids.*

Not dumb. Gorgeous. And yes, we all should.

CHAPTER 27

... *And They All Lived Happily Ever After*

ONE MORE THOUGHT at the end about why beginnings matter. Because it seems we might go back there at some point. Let me tell you about it this way.

I adore my husband. We have a terrific time together — we laugh, talk, travel, celebrate, commiserate, challenge and support each other. When we got married on a whim in Las Vegas in 2011 (after being together for nearly a dozen years) it was the most doubt-free decision I'd ever made. We're as solid as a rock, and it is all tremendous fun. I wouldn't have it any other way.

Also, this. One of my great pleasures is *Midsomer Murders*. It is a British television detective drama starring either John Nettles (original) or Neil Dudgeon (latest incarnation) as Detective Inspector Barnaby of Causton CID. Causton and the surrounding district is filthy with murders. Seriously, they average about five dead bodies per episode and the thing has been running for 20 years. I find it endlessly soothing. One hundred minutes at a time filled to bursting with middle-class white people killing each other over money and sex. They are all either privileged or eccentric or both, and largely unrelatable, so you don't feel invested and heartbroken as, one by one, they bump each other off. Stabbings and poisonings and quite a lot of being whacked around the head with something handy, like a shovel. Also, the village architecture is ye olde charming and the scenery is picturesque. When you hear foxes shrieking at the moon as a portent for some fresh killing, it's as familiar and comforting as the sound of a train way off in the distance at night.

Anyway, there was an episode where, in the opening scene, a middle-aged woman was found dead, face-down in a pond. Inspector Barnaby asked the local plod if her family had been notified yet. 'No, sir. It seems she lived alone in a cottage over by the Causton library.' And all I could think was, ah, how lovely that sounds. Peaceful. I bet that was a nice life. She would have had a cat. And I thought those things while the shot still lingered on her, face-down in the pond.

I'm just saying that sometimes we can fantasise about other lives, and imagine their simplicity. But here's the thing:

as complex and demanding as relationships might be, there is oodles of evidence that they are tremendously good for us. Studies suggest people in long-term, happy relationships are less likely to suffer strokes, heart disease or depression, they respond better to stress and heal more quickly.

More than this, in an interview in *Time* magazine in 2016, John Gottman, one of America's leading marriage researchers and educators, reported that the longer people are together, the more their sense of kindness returns. And this little gem: 'Our research is starting to reveal that in later life, your relationship becomes very much like it was during courtship.'

Which is a lovely full circle. Next time you need a little fantasy to ponder, try that. And in 30 years, if you hear of an elderly couple breaking into a yacht or having sex in an art gallery, you can be pretty sure it is Warren and Fay.

Glossary of Kiwi Words and Phrases

BECAUSE SO MUCH OF THIS BOOK is based on conversations with Kiwis, there are a few words and phrases that might be specific to New Zealand, and unfamiliar to people in other places. If you can't be arsed googling, this should help.

Duck-egg — a swollen bruise, which Tim Sandbrook uses as a verb in Chapter 8 when he says his ankle 'duck-egged'. Non-New Zealanders may be more familiar with 'goose-egg' as a bruise descriptor but in places like the Waikato there are more ducks than geese, hence the localised term.

Kiwi — our national emblem. A charming, nocturnal, flightless bird which, therefore, barely meets the requirements of being a bird. It gets its name from its call, which sounds like 'kee-wee'. Try it. Kiwi is also shorthand for 'New Zealander'.

Labour Weekend — other countries have Labour Day to celebrate the institution of the eight-hour working day, but in New Zealand we have a whole weekend. First celebrated in 1900 as a statutory holiday, it was Monday-ised in 1910 and falls on the fourth Monday in October. It is our first holiday after a long winter. This is the weekend we all plant our tomatoes, put away our woollies, and tail our lambs.

OE — Overseas Experience. What Kiwis call the year or years they bugger off to the other side of the world to work and play. (It is a generally accepted thing in New Zealand that people who live on islands should visit other islands.) Originally, the OE featured living in damp London squats, but these days is more likely to involve periods of couch surfing, and earning sufficient money to pay off their student loan. Eventually, most people come home — sometimes with partners and kids they have sourced elsewhere.

Whakapapa — the Māori concept of genealogy, which is a fundamental principle in the culture. A person reciting their whakapapa places themselves in the wider context of the people and the land they belong to and are connected with. It is a critical element in establishing your identity.

Whānau, hapū and iwi — very broadly, these Māori words translate to 'family, subtribe and tribe' though they are richer and more complex, emotionally and spiritually, than their English equivalents.

Wild and woolly — an expression commonly used in New Zealand to describe weather and coastlines, evocative of clouds of raw sheep's wool billowing all over the show.

ACKNOWLEDGEMENTS

I AM ENDLESSLY GRATEFUL to all of the people who offered their stories for this book. People who volunteered themselves, or were dobbed in by family and friends, or who let me bail them up in corridors, over lunches or after shows with my recorder in hand. (Though I like to think that most of them chased me rather than the other way around — you know how it goes.) People were remarkably generous with their time and their stories, their cups of tea and their cake.

I did a weird thing as I was writing: I found it helpful to have a picture of each couple sitting beside me as I told their story. Sometimes I had a photo they'd sent, or that I'd taken when I met them, but occasionally it required hunting them down on Facebook. Which might mean that out of the blue I'd wish them a happy birthday, or congratulate them on the birth of a grandchild, or ask if their leg was better. Apologies for coming across like a stalker. I will stop doing that now. Probably.

Special love and thanks to my mother and to Maeve, who, in between telling their stories and having them told, experienced the extraordinary grief of losing their One In Particular. I feel honoured that they let their stories with my father and with Declan continue to live on inside these pages.

Sometimes — not often — I have changed people's names and occupations to protect their privacy. It is a testament, I think, to how much their stories mean to them that they want other people to enjoy the narrative even if they don't want them to be able to identify who the characters are. I like to picture the anonymous couples being able to point at a chapter, or part of a chapter, and say quietly to the people closest to them, 'See these people? They are us.'

I owe a huge debt of gratitude to Professor Donna Rose Addis at the University of Auckland for being so bloody enthusiastic, and kind, and clear about all the science-y stuff to do with memory. It was a revelation, and I will never forget it. Encoded and retrieved.

Same goes for psychologist Sara Chatwin, who generously lent her expertise and effervescence to the whole thing, and reassured me that I was onto something.

Thanks also to the fabulous people at RNZ National, who helped me get the word out about the project, and forwarded emails from listeners to me whenever they turned up — especially Jim Mora, Julie Moffett, Simone Millar and Jesse Mulligan (who also turns up in one of the stories along with Ben Hurley — surprise!).

Warm thanks, too, to Anthony Dreaver, Dan Crozier, Patrick (Paddy) Davies, Kate Stone, Sandra Noakes, Finlay Macdonald and Jeremy Elwood for words of encouragement at just the right times. Aperol Spritz at mine at the earliest opportunity.